Relationship Compatibility Astrology for Love, Intimacy, & Business

GURMEET SINGH

Copyright © 2014 Gurmeet Singh

All rights reserved.

ISBN-13: 978-0-9960135-0-5

List Price $35.95

Printed by CreateSpace, An Amazon.com Company

PREFACE

Do you know how the time of your birth affects your destiny? Do you know if the ruling planets of your love partner have connection with certain houses in your natal astrology chart, then they will have a high degree of intimacy and love compatibility with you? Do you know if the ruling planets of your business partner have connection with certain houses in your natal astrology chart, then they can bring big financial gains for you in business? Look no further – because the key to finding your perfect love or business partner is in the stars! Now author Gurmeet Singh presents a new approach to Relationship Compatibility Astrology by presenting his research work in the field of astrology. This book gives information on certain important relationship compatibility issues such as Intimacy & Sexual Compatibility, Gay/Lesbian tendencies, cheating, separation, divorce, violent–criminal tendencies, longevity and health of spouse, business compatibility, with case studies. With acclaimed Astrologer Gurmeet Singh as your guide, you can harness your own destiny, and uncover revelations about yourself and your love or business partner that you may never have known before. This book can be used by straight as well as gay/lesbian readers.

GURMEET SINGH

WWW.VEDICNAKSHATRAS.COM

CONTENTS

	Acknowledgments	I
1	Relationship Compatibility Astrology Introduction	1
2	Astrology Houses And Relationship Compatibility	6
3	Sexual Compatibility	10
4	Cheating, Separation, and Divorce in Relationship	24
5	Gay, Lesbian Tendencies in the Astrology Chart	35
6	Longevity and Health of Spouse	55
7	Violent and Criminal Tendencies in the Astrology Chart	76
8	Business Compatibility	103

ACKNOWLEDGMENTS

Gurmeet,

Thank you for the detailed reading. I am very excited you are writing. The first Vedic astrologer i ever met was back in 1989. He wrote some beginners books on transits and jyotish charts. His delineations of my mahadasha at that time were generalized but helpful to me to understand the major period I was going through. And his books gave me general knowledge. But again I was only looking for deeper understanding of my purpose in life and my spiritual path.

But I never really looked to Jyotish for predictions. I had no faith in that until your readings all played out exactly as you read them. The emphasis on the nakshatras for finer understanding is a revelation. I cannot remember how I found you. Internet I suppose but it was my good fortune to do so. I am sure your books will illuminate the science for many professional astrologers as well as the novices like me.

If you plan your next trip to Houston I will arrange for you to do some readings. I have a few friends that would benefit from your talents right now. I hope you have a wonderful holiday.

1 RELATIONSHIP COMPATIBILITY ASTROLOGY INTRODUCTION

One of the best uses of astrology is in analyzing relationships. Astrology can help explain why we have the friends and partners we do, and how we get along with other people by noting areas of harmony and cooperation as well as possible stress and discord. Have you ever wondered why you are sexually attracted to someone? Do you ever wonder why you can't seem to get along with someone, despite your best efforts? The goal of this book is to help you understand how astrology affects Relationship Compatibility, and how you can apply the divine power of astrology to help you find a suitable Love Partner or a Business Partner with Relationship Compatibility. Is it important to find a partner who you are compatible with in every aspect of life? There is no single person on the planet you will be compatible with in every way. If you look for just one person to meet all your needs, then you are setting yourself up for a big disappointment. When it comes to relationship compatibility for Love, it is so important to find someone with that special chemistry, passion, and attraction. They should simply care for each other – to consistently like, respect and support each other as autonomous individuals. They should have fun together and really enjoy the time they spend together. Relationships thrive when two people share companionship and activities. However, a couple doesn't have to have every interest in common. While in Relationship

Compatibility for Business, it is important to find a Business Partner who will bring Financial Prosperity, and success in Business. At the same time the person is reliable, honest, and trustworthy. We can learn a lot about ourselves and others through an exploration of positions, placements, and aspects in natal astrology charts. There are specific things to look for in the astrology chart that will help shed light on individual temperaments, preferences, styles, love, and sex life.

In a long term relationship or marriage, the vast majority of the time couples are together, they are sharing a practical day to day life together, such as raising children, working, managing a home, cooking and cleaning, shopping, being with friends and family. If couples are not compatible in these areas then inevitably tensions emerge, and too often relationships fall apart. That is why when people are divorcing they'll say "We have nothing in common". So what do you think? How important do you think compatibility is for a long term relationship? Counseling doesn't work, if your astrology charts are not compatible. Many people talk about finding their "soul mate". Whether or not this is possible, astrology can reveal special connections between people. Which component in a romantic relationship is more important: attraction or compatibility? While many would argue in favor of compatibility, but I would say it is attraction that can lead to a healthy, long-lasting and loving relationship. Attraction may create or lead to Compatibility, but Compatibility alone is not enough to keep a man and woman together. In this book we use Astrology to explore these special love connections (Attraction and Compatibility) between different people.

Is there such a thing as "true love?" The reason I ask is that my observations of the world today indicate that there are more people getting divorced, getting cheated on, and breaking up than there are happy couples that are in love and stay in love. I mean, are humans mentally and physically capable of staying in love with someone and being faithful to each other? In the absence of love, we have fallen back on compatibility as the basis for relationships. And in doing so we have forgotten perhaps the greatest secret of relationships--namely, that love creates compatibility. Why is relationship compatibility so important? Because people are simply not happy when they're with someone they're not compatible with.

Do you have a good relationship compatibility with your

RELATIONSHIP COMPATIBILITY ASTROLOGY

Partner? Believe it or not, your relationship compatibility determines whether your relationship will be a lifetime of love and happiness or a complete disaster. Did you know that incompatibility between intimate partners contributes to 78% of break ups, and is at the core of all Relationship problems? Learn here about relationship compatibility astrology and how to know who you're compatible with using Vedic Astrology techniques.

There are various astrological systems in use, for assessing compatibility between two people for love, romance, sex, and for Business Partnerships. Westerners compare the Venus signs of the two Partners to find a love match. Traditional Vedic Astrology uses a system involving matching the moons to determine if the charts of two people are in agreement with each other for love, romance, and sex. This is known as the Kuta System. The Kuta System compares the two astrology charts, in which a score out of 36 points is given, based on matching the Moons in the two charts, and the maximum possible score is 35. It compares how well the Moon constellation (Nakshatra) and Moon sign of one partner aligns with the Moon constellation (Nakshatra) and Moon sign of the other Partner. If the final score is 18 or more the match is said to be favorable. A score of 25 or higher is said to indicate a very good match. Another technique that is very popular among both Western and Vedic Astrologers is the reading of the two charts together, by matching the signs and overlying one chart on top of the other.. This can relate how the energies of the different planets resonate with each other, by determining planetary aspects and conjunctions.

In my opinion none of these systems gave me accurate results. I have seen happy marriages where the Venus signs didn't match or the Kuta Score was low. I have also seen cases where the marriages ended in Divorce but the Kuta score was high or the Venus signs were compatible. The astrology compatibility or relationship compatibility astrology predictions that you read in magazines, and internet sites where the astrologers / psychics compare your zodiac signs to find astrology compatibility or relationship compatibility or business compatibility do not work in real life. Because billions of people around the world are born in a particular month and they could all relate to a particular zodiac sign but they all cannot be compatible with you for love, romance or business. Even people born in a particular month or on a particular day having same zodiac sign could be completely different in their personality, nature and habits. Then how can they be compatible with you for love romance or business just using the zodiac signs.

Beyond the astrological twelve signs most are familiar with; Aries, Taurus, Gemini, etc., in Vedic astrology there are also twenty-seven divisions within them called Constellations (Nakshatras). These nakshatras reveal the most about your nature and temperament, and it's these nakshatras that are the most important when looking at how you relate to others. Further it divides each Constellation / Star / Nakshatra division into further 9 subdivisions called 'SUBS'. These sub divisions are not equal divisions, as per the Vimshottari Dashas Divisions System. Find out what areas are going to be more work and what seems to bring the two of you together by having a Compatibility Reading done. This unique and fascinating reading will rate your physical, emotional, sexual, psychological and spiritual compatibilities as well as look at the longevity of the relationship. It will unveil if the two of you will be better able to make the relationship what you want it to be, without attracting obstacles to your goals for each other. Your relationship compatibility determines whether your relationship will be a lifetime of love and happiness or a complete disaster. Learn here how to use Relationship Compatibility Astrology to know who you're compatible with.

Natal Vedic Astrology, Jyotish concerns largely with the birth of a human being. A Horoscope is made out for the moment of birth for the particular place of birth (latitude and longitude being taken into consideration) and from such a Horoscope one can read all events which he or she desires to know. Here not only the native's character, temperament and peculiarities may be judged but also his longevity, condition of health, finance and fortune, marriage, birth of children, and also prosperity or adversity.

The Horoscope or the radix is the fountain from which springs events in one's life. What is promised in the radical chart in accordance with one's karma will unfold itself in the form of good or bad events at some time or other in one's life. Hindu sages have devised several methods to predict the time of events, of which Udu (nakshatra) Dasa system propounded by Maharishi Parasara is most widely followed. The effects of the planets do not merely depend upon their lordship, occupation or association but much more on their situation in the various nakshatras and sub divisions called subs. The Vedic Astrology system that we are using for analysis in this book uses KP Ayanamshas as opposed to Lahiri Ayanamshas mostly used in Vedic Astrology. The difference between the two is about 6 minutes. This system uses Cusps that is house/ bhav beginnings like Western System, as opposed to Vedic System which uses House Centres i.e. Bhav Madhyas. This system uses Placidus House system. The planet in it's dasha gives results as per it's Nakshtra-Lord (Star-Lord) rather than the planet itself. Hence Planet represents the SOURCE, that Planet's Star-Lord represents the EFFECTS, RESULTS and that Planet's Sub gives idea of the FINAL DIRECTION of that result. Vedic Astrology is a powerful predictive science, but it is not 100% accurate due to certain factors such as the inaccuracy of the true birth time and some proportion of human error. The information obtained from this book should be used as a guideline or roadmap. Each person ultimately remains fully responsible for their behavior, judgments, actions, and decision making process. Readers may use the information from this book according to their own best interests, completely at their sole discretion.

2 ASTROLOGY HOUSES AND RELATIONSHIP COMPATIBILITY

There are twelve houses in the Vedic Astrology Chart. Each house influences certain matters of our life. The 2nd, 5th, 7th, and 11th houses in the astrology chart promote happiness, love, sex, and romance in the relationship.

SECOND HOUSE: The second house in the astrology chart is the house of money. It represents the financial prosperity of the native. This house represents the person's bank balance, the degree of prosperity they will enjoy and the individual's worldly attainments. The second house also deals with the family of the native. It includes all close relatives. When a person is in a relationship or they get married, there is extension to their family. The spouse and children are part of the family, and the family is represented by the second house in the astrology chart. The second house is also the house of speech, and communication skills. It represents the native's ability to express their thoughts. The second house along with the 5 house has to be considered to determine whether one has the aptitude for music.

FIFTH HOUSE: Fifth house in the astrology chart is the house of love, romance, love affairs, sex, intercourse, rape, physical pleasures, love marriage, physical attraction between opposite sexes and pregnancy in the native's life. The native's love life, sexual enjoyment, love affairs, and pregnancy etc are judged from the analysis of the 5th house in the astrology chart. The successes or failures in love affairs are measured by the analysis of the 5th house. Love affairs/attraction outside marriage fall under the domain of 5th house. Fifth house is the house of the progeny. It represents whether one will have children or not. Fifth house also represents entertainment business, artistic talents, and sports. Connection of 1st house, 5th house and 10th house lords can make the person a movie star or a sports figure. The person can also become a singer or musician if the 2nd house is also involved in this configuration. Fifth house also represents speculative affairs, gambling, betting, and stock exchange etc. Fifth house connection also gives good health to the native. As it negates all health issues that are represented by the 6th house in the astrology chart.

SEVENTH HOUSE: Marriage is represented by the 7th house in the astrology chart. The 7th house represents all legal ties, desire, love, kama, house of union, cohabitation, legal bondage, marriage etc. All romantic or business partnerships, contracts etc. in life are represented by the 7th house in the astrology chart. The marriage can be a love marriage if there is a connection between the 5th house and the 7th house in their astrology charts. If it is connected with Rahu or Ketu, then the love affair or marriage is with a person belonging to a different culture. The degree of success achieved through a love partnership or business partnership is shown by this house. Seventh house represents people that come in contact with the native in their daily life or with whom the native deals in any manner. Native's wife, spouse, girl friend, friends, co-workers, boss, subordinates, competitors, and enemies etc are all represented by the 7th house in the astrology chart.

ELEVENTH HOUSE: Eleventh house is the house of friendships, fulfillment of desires, passion, and success in all undertakings. It also represents wealth, riches, and all kinds of profits/gains in life. The eleventh house governs success in all undertakings, whether it is in love, business or profession. Accumulation of wealth in astrology chart is indicated by the eleventh house. Eleventh house also represents pleasures, profit, prosperity, and permanent tie or friendship. The eleventh house stands for lasting friendship and intimacy that may end in marriage. Eleventh house also indicates pleasures with opposite sex without actually contracting marriage.

The 4th, 6th, 8th, 12th, and Badhaka houses in the astrology chart are detrimental to happiness, love, sex, and romance in the relationship.

FOURTH HOUSE: Fourth house relates to one's home, residence, mother, car etc. Fourth house also shows landed or immovable properties, and whether one will have vehicles in their life time. This house also represents qualifications of the native. While the fourth house may help in acquiring landed properties, cars, education etc., but fourth house negates love, romance, pregnancy, and sex in the person's life as 4th house is 12th house to 5th house of love, romance, sex, and pregnancy. In other words planets connected with 4th house negate 5th house matters. During the dasha / bhukti of planet connected with the 4th house the love, romance, and sex is not that exciting. The person has hard time having a child.

SIXTH HOUSE: Sixth house represents diseases or is known as the 'house of sickness'. This is an important house for those who deal with the treatment of sick people, such as nurses and doctors. Sixth house also represents one's daily job or work. Sixth house also helps you to raise a funding or loan from a Bank or investors. But sixth house also represents divorce / temporary separation, and lonely time in life. Sixth house negates marriage as it is 12th house to the 7th house of marriage in the astrology chart. Sixth house brings violence in a relationship if malefic planets such as Mars, Rahu, Ketu and Saturn are in the 6th house in the astrology chart. Sixth house brings coldness in marriage or relationship. Sixth house plays a very important role when the spouse of the native cheats on them in their marriage or relationship. During the dasha /bhukti of a planet connected with 6th house the person finds it difficult to meet people or start a new relationship or get married. If the person is already married then during the dasha / bhukti of planets connected with 6th house either the marriage or relationship ends or there could be a temporary separation due to some family or job circumstances.

EIGHTH HOUSE: Eighth house represents one's longevity or span of life. This house is also called the 'house of death'. It is related to inheritance, wills, lotteries, and legacies. Accidents, surgeries, fine, punishment, suffering, disappointments, misfortunes, scandals, misery, ill repute, insult, defeat, imprisonment, and court matters also fall under the portfolio of the eighth house. Eighth house is related to their unearned wealth or share of profit. Eighth house represents the money that belongs to other people as it is 2nd house to the 7th house. Seventh house represents people that come in contact with the native in their daily life. Eighth house denotes fights, quarrels, and arguments in relationship or marriage, but it will not end the marriage or relationship. Separation or divorce is always represented by the 6th and the 12th houses in the astrology chart.

TWELFTH HOUSE Twelfth house deals with losses, expenses, purchases, investments, donations, and charity etc. Twelfth house also represents hospitalization, imprisonment, secret activities, destruction, loss, living in unknown place, misfortunes, poverty, obstacles, secret enemies, deception, and repayment of loan, if one has borrowed money. Twelfth house indicates life in a foreign country, change of place or change in surroundings and environment. Twelfth house denotes divorce or separation in marriage or relationship. During the dasha / bhukti of planets connected with 6th house and 12th house, the romantic or business partnership / relationship ends.

BADHAKA HOUSE: Badhaka house is the worst house for all matters, including relationship matters in one's life. Planets connected with Badhaka house, 8th house and 12th house at same time cause suicide, murder, accidents, disease, disgrace in profession etc. Planets in the nakshatras of the Badhaka Planet become more evil than the Badhaka Planet. Planets in the constellation of the occupants of the Bhadhakasthana, are the strongest evils, next the occupants of Bhadhakasthana, next those in the constellation of the lords of the Bhadhakasthana, and lastly the lords of those evil houses. When Rahu/Ketu are in the sign of, aspected or conjoined by Bhadaka Lord, then extreme harmful results are to be predicted. But if Badhaka Lord is deposited in good nakshatras, then it gives very good results during its dasha / bhukti. 11th house to chara rasis or movable signs (Aries, Cancer, Libra, Capricorn), 9th house to sthira rasi or fixed signs(Taurus, Leo, Scorpio, Aquarius), and 7th house to Ubhaya rasis or common signs(Gemini, Virgo, Sagittarius, Pisces) are badhaka sthanas or badhaka houses.

3 SEXUAL COMPATIBILITY

How do you define Sexual Compatibility?
There is no single definition for sexual compatibility. Either Sexual Compatibility is there or it is not. You can't control who you love. Sexual Compatibility with a partner is related to sexual satisfaction, such that the more sexually compatible you are, the more sexually satisfied you are. Satisfying sex brings Sexual Compatibility, and Sexual Compatibility brings Relationship Compatibility. Sexual Compatibility is so unpredictable. You may be physically attracted to someone, does not mean you will be sexually compatible with them. Sex could be completely boring with them. You may have incredible sex with someone, you have not really been that attracted, because you both are sexually compatible.

How important is Sexual Compatibility?
Sexual Compatibility is very important for love relationship and marriage. Sexual Compatibility is the foundation of a long-term loving relationship. Sexual Compatibility is what holds couples together in a love relationship or marriage for many, many years. Marriages or love relationships cannot survive if the couples do not have Sexual Compatibility. In other words, Sexual Compatibility is a deal breaker, in most love relationships and marriages. I tell everyone who will listen to me, that sex can make or break a relationship. Of course, sex should not be the most important factor in a relationship, but it is, and you and your partner must be

sexually compatible. It is not shameful to consider Sexual Compatibility an important factor of your relationship. Sexual Compatibility plays a very important role in a healthy marriage and love relationship. The area of Sexual Compatibility is sometimes completely forgotten when choosing a mate. I have always wondered why many men and women seem to put sexual compatibility low on their list of priorities. During my Relationship Compatibility Astrology Readings with my clients, I always tell them to put long lasting Sexual Compatibility as one of the top things they want in a love relationship and marriage. If you make Sexual Compatibility as one of your top things in a relationship, then finding out whether you are sexually compatible will be very important to you. Possible compatibility issues are, mismatched sex drives, mismatched sexual preferences, and sexual orientation (marrying a gay person when you are straight). Also there can be a mismatch of physical bodies, one partner could be very tall or heavy compared to the other partner, and also how your bodies / genitals fit together can be a mismatch too. Some of you think that sexual compatibility won't matter once you are married. In my opinion they are so wrong. Would you be in a relationship or marriage with a Partner with very little Sexual Compatibility, for the rest of your life? My guess is probably not. Sexual compatibility is just that important part of a love relationship and marriage. The unique thing about sexual Compatibility is that it creates Relationship compatibility between two people who would otherwise have nothing in common. Perhaps it is only when the sexual side of a relationship isn't going very well, that partners perceive they aren't sexually compatible with their partner in terms of their sexual preferences. Couples leave each other because they have lost their sexual compatibility or it was never there in the first place. Keep in mind sex is a big part of marriage and needs to be worked on until the end. Believe it or not, your sexual compatibility determines whether your relationship will be a lifetime of love and happiness or a complete disaster. So my advice to anyone who is considering a long term monogamous commitment to another: check out your sexual compatibility.

How Astrology can help you find a sexually compatible love partner?

In my work with gay, lesbian and straight couples, the issue of sexual compatibility comes up frequently. This is because Sexual

Compatibility matters in Love Relationships. More frequently my clients ask questions such as, 'Is this person a good sexual partner for me?', 'Am I Sexually Compatible with my current Partner?', 'How can I assess my Sexual Compatibility with a future partner?'. Most couples tying the knot don't want to wait until the honeymoon to know if things are going to work in the bedroom, and would agree that having sex before marriage is an important way to establish if there's a basic level of sexual compatibility. One obvious way to find out if you are sexually compatible is to sleep with the person, that way you know if it's a fit or not, if you like it or don't. However, this is not usually the best way especially if you want to give true attraction and true love a chance to reveal itself. Whichever way you choose to do it, and no matter how much you love somebody, you'll have a difficult time moving past the problems sexual incompatibility creates in your relationship if you do not deal with it openly, truthfully and honestly. Can one determine if they are sexually compatible with their potential spouse without having sex, or should they try sleeping with their partner so as to know if they are sexually compatible or not? Since many people will not want to wait that long to know if they have found a sexually compatible mate or not. How can you know if you are sexually compatible with your spouse? Where and when do you discover your sexual compatibleness? Considering the extent to which sexual compatibility contributes to satisfaction in our relationships, it is somewhat surprising that there isn't more research done on this topic in the field of Astrology. Western Astrology uses Zodiac Signs or comparison of Venus signs, to find Sexual Compatibility which in my opinion doesn't work most of the times. Billions of people are born in a particular month, they could all relate to a particular zodiac sign, and they all cannot be sexually compatible with you. Most Vedic Astrologers use Kuta System to establish Sexual Compatibility between couples, but it fails too. Most of the times, we find that couples with low Kuta Score are happily married, but couples with high Kuta Score are divorced. I have done extensive research on Sexual Compatibility between couples during my career as a Professional Astrologer. I can tell by looking at astrology charts of two potential partners (Gay or Straight) if they have a high degree of Sexual Compatibility between them or not. I can also tell my single clients (Gay or Straight), if their astrology chart is good for love life. When they can find a Sexually Compatible Partner in their life? How the astrology chart of the potential future partner should like, to find the true Sexual Compatibility. Are you involved in a relationship that you are hoping will become sexual one day, but it hasn't advanced to that level of intimacy? Are you wondering if the delay is natural or a sign of disinterest in your love interest? If you're lucky enough to have the information, you can bring the date, place and time of birth of your lover to me and I will tell you the answer.

When two partners are together for love, romance, and sex
 1. There is friendship between them, and the friendship is represented by the 11th house in their astrology charts.
 2. There is sex, passion between them which can lead to pregnancy. The sex, passion, and pregnancy is represented by the 5th house in their astrology charts.
 3. if they decide to get married, then their marriage is represented by the 7th house in their astrology charts. The 7th house represents legal ties. All romantic or business partnerships, contracts etc. in life are represented by the 7th house in the astrology chart. The marriage can be a love marriage if there is a connection between the 5th house and the 7th house in their astrology charts if it is connected with Rahu or Ketu, then the love affair or marriage is with a person belonging to a different culture.
 4. After marriage their family is represented by the 2nd house in their astrology chart.
 So the 2nd, 5th, 7th, and 11th houses promote happiness, love and romance in the marriage / relationship.

RULING PLANETS: The Ruling Planets in any astrology chart consists of the following:
 1: Your ascendant sign lord in your astrology chart
 2. Your ascendant nakshatra lord in your astrology chart
 3. Your Moon sign lord in your astrology chart
 4. Your Moon nakshatra lord in your astrology chart
 5. The planet representing the day when you were born
 The ascendant sign lord and the ascendant nakshatra lord are the most important planets, when I do Sexual Compatibility Analysis for my clients. Next comes, the Moon sign lord and the Moon nakshatra lord.

GOLDEN RULE TO FIND OUT THE SEXUAL COMPATIBILITY WITH YOUR LOVER:

If the ruling planets in your astrology chart, at the time of your birth have a strong connection with the 5th house in your lover's astrology chart, then your lover will be madly drawn towards you for sex, love, and romance because your ruling planets are activating the 5th house of love, and sex in your lover's astrology chart. This means you are good for the 5th house matters for your lover, and that is bed pleasures, satisfying and good sex. Your lover will find a strong Sexual Compatibility with you. Your lover will not be able to leave you easily, because you are the one who can fulfill your lover's sexual needs, because your ruling planets are activating their 5th house of sex in their astrology chart. If the ruling planets of your lover's astrology chart at the time of their birth have a strong connection with the 5th house in your astrology chart, then you will also be madly drawn towards your lover for sex, love and romance. This is a perfect Sexual Compatibility match, where the ruling planets of both love partners at the time of their birth are activating each other's 5th house of sex and bed pleasures in their astrology charts. They will meet each other for the first time when either one will be going through the mahadasha /bhukti/ anthara of the planets connected with 2nd, 5th, 7th, and 11th houses in their astrology charts. Such cases are very rare. I have seen such cases about 5% of the time, during my career as a Professional career.

Most of the time Sexual Compatibility is a one way street, you can say. Where Partner A is madly in love with the Partner B in a relationship for sex, because the Partner B's ruling planets at the time of their birth are activating the 5th house of bed pleasures and sex in the Partner A's astrology chart, but not vice versa. In this example Partner A is madly in love with Partner B, and thinks that Partner B is Sexually Compatible. But Partner B is not madly in love with Partner A, and thinks differently.

We also have cases where the Partner A and Partner B's ruling planets at the time of their birth have no connection with the 5th house of bed pleasures and sex or the 7th house of relationships in each other's astrology charts, and they are miserable in their love relationship or marriage. In my opinion there is no Sexual Compatibility in such cases. I have seen such cases when people go for arranged marriages in certain cultures.

RELATIONSHIP COMPATIBILITY ASTROLOGY

The GOLDEN RULE is if your potential partner's ascendant lord and ascendant nakshatra lord are connected strongly with your 5th house in your astrology chart then that person can fulfill your sexual desires. If the potential partner's moon sign and moon nakshatra lord also have connection with your 5th house then it is even better. You will be deeply in love with that person, as the potential partner's ruling planets are activating your 5th house of sexual pleasures. In this case you will not be able to leave this person as their ruling planets are activating your house of sex. But if both partners are activating each other's 5th house then the sexual compatibility is very high between the two love partners for bed pleasures. The Golden Rule for Sexual Compatibility works for both Straight and Gay couples.

MARRIAGE COMPATIBILITY: When you want to study the Marriage Compatibility with your love Partner, you need to include the 7th house analysis as well from astrology charts of both love partners. Marriage is represented by the 7th house in the astrology chart. The 7th house represents all legal ties, desire, love, kama, house of union, cohabitation, legal bondage, marriage etc. The marriage can be a love marriage if there is a connection between the 5th house lord and the 7th house lord in their respective astrology charts. If they are connected with Rahu or Ketu, then the love affair or marriage is with a person belonging to a different culture. Seventh house represents people that come in contact with the native in their daily life or with whom the native deals in any manner. Native's wife, spouse, girl friend, friends, co-workers, boss, subordinates, competitors, and enemies etc are all represented by the 7th house in the astrology chart.

In the girl's chart, lord of 7th house should not be in any way connected to 6-12 houses in the boy's chart. Similarly in a boy's chart the lord of 7th house should not be in any way connected to 6-12 houses of the girl's chart. Also the lord of 7th should not be stationed in the 6th or 12th house or in the stars of 6th or 12th house. Therefore, relevant to marriage matters we should take care to observe, that the 7th lord of the girl's chart should not occupy stars of houses in the boy's chart that are detrimental to marriage matters, and vice versa. The 7th cusp of the native will guide you to tell the lagna cusp of the life partner, would be husband or wife.

If the ruling planets of love partner A at birth be the significators of 6, 8 or 12 and not of 1, 5, or 11 in the horoscope of love partner B, then A will not be compatible with love partner B for sex and marriage. During the joint period of the significators of 6, 8, or 12 in the horoscope of love partner B, B will not feel happy with love partner A. If the ruling planets of the love partner A are the strong significators of 12 and 6 in the horoscope of love partner B, then it leads to divorce. For marriage study the cusp lord of 2, 7, and 11 houses. It they are the significators of 2, 5, 7, 11 then marriage is possible. If they are the significators of 1, 6, 10, and 12, then it indicates absence of married life. You should never be in a relationship or marriage with a love partner, whose ruling planets at the time of their birth are connected with the Badhaka house in your astrology chart or vice versa, as it can lead to violence in a relationship.

We will do couple of case studies that will address your question 'What kind of person will have sexual compatibility with me?'

CASE STUDY 1 FOR SEXUAL COMPATIBILITY

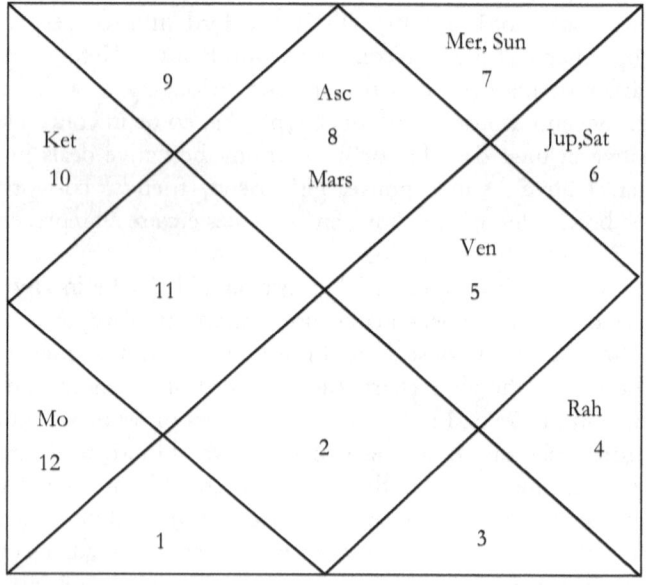

This person is a Scorpio ascendant with ascendant degree at 15 degrees and 22 minutes in Scorpio sign. For Scorpio ascendant Jupiter is a very auspicious planet as it rules 2nd house of money and family, and 5th house of bed pleasures and sex. Planets connected with Jupiter will also be considered in determining Sexual Compatibility, as they will also be good for bed pleasures. Mercury rules the 8th house and 11th house and it is positioned in 12th house in Vishaka nakshatra ruled by 5th house lord Jupiter. Jupiter from Virgo also aspects Ketu in Capricorn by its 5th aspect, and 9th house lord Moon by its 7th aspect. Jupiter is in conjunction with 3rd, and 4th house lord Saturn. The lord of 7th and 12th house is Venus, and Venus is very close to the 10th house cusp, in its own nakshatra P Phalguni in Leo sign.

Planets connected with the 5th house – Jupiter, Mercury, Ketu, Saturn and Moon. Planets connected with the 7th house – Venus. From this list we omit Moon as Moon is a Badhaka Planet for Scorpio ascendant. We keep Mercury although it rules the 8th house, because Mercury is in 5th house lord Jupiter's Vishaka nakshatra. We also omit Saturn as it rules 4th house which negates 5th house matters (sex, bed pleasures, pregnancy), and Saturn is in Badhaka Planet Moon's Hasta Nakshatra. We keep Venus as it rules 7th house of marriage or legal tie.

Final list of Planets for Sexual Compatibility: Jupiter, Ketu, Venus, and Mercury. Pisces sign falls in 5th house, and there are three nakshatras in Pisces Sign – 0 degrees to 3 degrees 20 minutes is Jupiter's own nakshatra P Bhadrapad, 3 degrees 20 minutes to 16 degrees 40 minutes is Saturn's nakshatra U. Bhadrapad, and 16 degrees 40 minutes to 30 degrees is Mercury's nakshatra Revati. This person will be sexually compatible with a love partner, whose lagna or the ascendant according to Vedic Astrology is between 0 and 3 degrees 20 minutes in Pisces or between 16 degrees 40 minutes and 30 degrees in Pisces sign. This person can meet such Sexually Compatible person when they are going through mahadasha, bhukti or anthara of Jupiter, Ketu, or Mercury in their lifetime.

The other sign ruled by 5th house lord Jupiter is Sagittarius that falls in 2nd house of family. Sagittarius sign has three nakshatras – 0 degrees to 13 degrees 20 minutes is Mula nakshatra ruled by Ketu, 13 degrees 20 minutes to 26 degrees 40 minutes is Purvashadha nakshatra ruled by Venus, and 26 degrees 40 minutes to 30 degrees is Uttarashadha nakshatra ruled by Sun. This person will also be sexually compatible with a love partner, whose lagna or the ascendant according to Vedic Astrology is between 0 and 13 degrees 20 minutes in Sagittarius or between 13 degrees 20 minutes and 26 degrees 40 minutes in Sagittarius sign. Taurus lagna for this person is good for marriage, but is average for Sexual Compatibility. This person can meet such Sexually Compatible person when they are going through mahadasha, bhukti or anthara of Jupiter, Ketu or Venus in their lifetime.

I will not recommend Libra ascendant ruled by Venus, although Vishaka nakshatra ruled by Jupiter falls in the last 10 degrees in Libra sign, because Libra sign falls in the evil 12th house of loss, and hidden enemies. In the same manner I will not recommend Gemini lagna, although Purnavashu nakshatra ruled by Jupiter falls in the last 10 degrees in Gemini sign, because Gemini sign falls in the evil 8th house of loss, and disappointments.

PLANET	LONGITUDE	NAKSHATRA
ASCENDANT	15 Sc 22' 01.30"	ANURADHA
SUN	4 Li 59' 11.68"	CHITRA
MOON	4 Pi 25' 38.93"	U BHADRAPAD
MARS	13 Sc 18' 13.86"	ANURADHA
MERCURY	26 Li 19' 03.43"	VISHAKA
JUPITER	5 Vi 23' 04.76"	U PHALGUNI
VENUS	26 Le 06' 15.36"	P PHALGUNI
SATURN(R)	10 Vi 12' 18.84"	HASTA
RAHU	22 Cn 47' 56.96"	ASLESHA
KETU	22 Cp 47' 56.96"	SHRAVANA

RELATIONSHIP COMPATIBILITY ASTROLOGY

House	Cusp	Middle	End	Planets in it
1ST	15 Sc 22' 01.30"	1 Sg 18' 50.97"	17 Sg 15' 40.65"	ASC
2ND	17 Sg 15' 40.65"	5 Cp 13' 15.20"	23 Cp 10' 49.75"	KETU
3RD	23 Cp 10' 49.75"	10 Aq 55' 49.91"	28 Aq 40' 50.07"	
4TH	28 Aq 40' 50.07"	13 Pi 50' 59.45"	29 Pi 01' 08.84"	MOON
5TH	29 Pi 01' 08.84"	11 Ar 25' 32.03"	23 Ar 49' 55.21"	
6TH	23 Ar 49' 55.21"	4 Ta 35' 58.25"	15 Ta 22' 01.30"	
7TH	15 Ta 22' 01.30"	1 Ge 18' 50.97"	17 Ge 15' 40.65"	
8TH	17 Ge 15' 40.65"	5 Cn 13' 15.20"	23 Cn 10' 49.75"	RAHU
9TH	23 Cn 10' 49.75"	10 Le 55' 49.91"	28 Le 40' 50.07"	VENUS
10TH	28 Le 40' 50.07"	13 Vi 50' 59.45"	29 Vi 01' 08.84"	JUP, SAT
11TH	29 Vi 01' 08.84"	11 Li 25' 32.03"	23 Li 49' 55.21"	SUN
12TH	23 Li 49' 55.21"	4 Sc 35' 58.25"	15 Sc 22' 01.30"	MER, MARS

CASE STUDY 2 FOR SEXUAL COMPATIBILITY

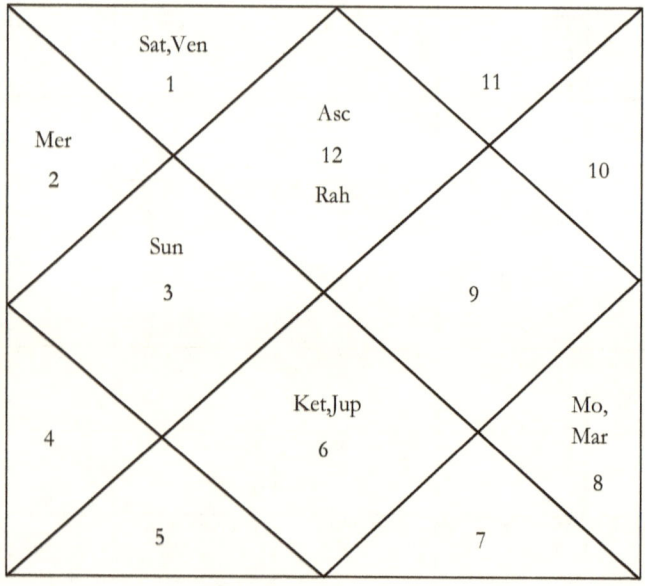

This person is a Pisces ascendant according to Vedic Astrology, with ascendant degree at 22 degrees 47 minutes in Pisces sign ruled by Jupiter. For Pisces ascendant, the three auspicious planets are Moon (5th house lord), Mars (2nd and 9th house lord) and Jupiter (1st and 10th house lord). These three auspicious planets Moon, Mars, and Jupiter are aspecting the 7th house of marriage or relationship lord Mercury in Taurus sign in the natal astrology chart. This makes the astrology chart very auspicious for marriage or love relationship. Mercury is not a friendly planet for Pisces ascendant, as it rules the 7th house, a Badhaka house for Pisces ascendant. But in this astrology chart the 7th house lord Mercury is in 5th house of bed pleasures and sex lord Moon's Rohini nakshatra in Taurus sign, and the 5th house lord Moon and 7th house lord Mercury are aspecting each other, very good for love marriage. In this astrology chart Planets connected with 5th house lord Moon will also be considered in determining Sexual Compatibility, as they will also be good for bed pleasures.

Planets connected with the 5th house – Moon, Mercury, Mars (Mars is conjunct Moon). Planets connected with the 7th house = Mercury, Ketu (in Mercury sign), Moon, Mars (Mercury aspects Mars)

Final List of planets for Sexual Compatibility: Moon, Mercury, Mars, Ketu. Cancer sign falls in 5th house, and there are three nakshatras in Cancer Sign – 0 degrees to 3 degrees 20 minutes is Jupiter's nakshatra Purnavasu, 3 degrees 20 minutes to 16 degrees 40 minutes is Saturn's nakshatra Pushyami, and 16 degrees 40 minutes to 30 degrees is Mercury's nakshatra Aslesha. This person will be sexually compatible with a love partner, whose lagna or the ascendant according to Vedic Astrology is between 16 degrees 40 minutes and 30 degrees in Cancer sign, this is where Aslesha Nakshatra ruled by 7th lord Mercury lies in the Cancer sign ruled by 5th house of bed pleasures lord Moon. This person will also be compatible for Marriage with a love partner, whose lagna or the ascendant according to Vedic Astrology is between 16 degrees 40 minutes and 30 degrees in Jyeshta nakshatra ruled by Mercury in Scorpio sign ruled by 2nd and 9th lord Mars.

I will not recommend Virgo ascendant ruled by Mercury for the love partner, although Hasta nakshatra ruled by Moon falls in the Virgo sign ruled by Mercury, because Virgo sign falls in the evil 7th house, a Badhaka house for Pisces ascendant.

GURMEET SINGH

PLANET	LONGITUDE	NAKSHATRA
ASCENDANT	22 Pi 47' 07.47"	REVATI
SUN	12 Ge 44' 51.21"	ARDRA
MOON	14 Sc 49' 14.17"	ANURADHA
MARS	11 Sc 17' 29.23"	ANURADHA
MERCURY	22 Ta 59' 29.80"	ROHINI
JUPITER	4 Vi 41' 05.75"	U PHALGUNI
VENUS	29 Ar 23' 11.71"	KRITTIKA
SATURN(R)	13 Ar 29' 27.89"	BHARANI
RAHU	1 Pi 50' 35.61"	P BHADRAPAD
KETU	1 Vi 50' 35.61"	U PHALGUNI

House	Cusp	Middle	End	Planets in it
1ST	22 Pi 47' 07.47"	10 Ar 04' 25.27"	27 Ar 21' 43.07"	SAT
2ND	27 Ar 21' 43.07"	10 Ta 29' 28.48"	23 Ta 37' 13.90"	VENUS, MER
3RD	23 Ta 37' 13.90"	5 Ge 19' 14.60"	17 Ge 01' 15.29"	SUN
4TH	17 Ge 01' 15.29"	29 Ge 26' 15.82"	11 Cn 51' 16.35"	
5TH	11 Cn 51' 16.35"	27 Cn 13' 50.43"	12 Le 36' 24.52"	

RELATIONSHIP COMPATIBILITY ASTROLOGY

6TH	12 Le 36' 24.52"	2 Vi 41' 46.00"	22 Vi 47' 07.47"	JUP, KET
7TH	22 Vi 47' 07.47"	10 Li 04' 25.27"	27 Li 21' 43.07"	
8TH	27 Li 21' 43.07"	10 Sc 29' 28.48"	23 Sc 37' 13.90"	MOON, MARS
9TH	23 Sc 37' 13.90"	5 Sg 19' 14.60"	17 Sg 01' 15.29"	
10TH	17 Sg 01' 15.29"	29 Sg 26' 15.82"	11 Cp 51' 16.35"	
11TH	11 Cp 51' 16.35"	27 Cp 13' 50.43"	12 Aq 36' 24.52"	
12TH	12 Aq 36' 24.52"	2 Pi 41' 46.00"	22 Pi 47' 07.47"	RAH

4 CHEATING, SEPARATION, AND DIVORCE IN RELATIONSHIP

In the USA alone, tens of millions of people cheat on their primary relationship partners. Cheating is very, very common. If you haven't experienced it yet, there's a good chance you eventually will. Most of the time cheating does occur, the other spouse doesn't know about it, with women being in the dark slightly more often than men. The big game-changer here is the Internet. Most people have flirted online at one point or another. Many people both men and women had real sex as a result of a connection that began online. In this chapter we'll explore how Relationship Compatibility Astrology can help you to know when and why a love partner will cheat in your relationship/marriage. I am going to discuss the Astrology techniques that can help you know when you can potentially become a victim of cheating, if you are already in a committed relationship or marriage. In other words, Relationship Compatibility Astrology can indicate the cheating tendencies in your astrology chart as well as your love partner's astrology chart. But if you follow the astrology information I presented in my previous chapter on 'Sexual Compatibility', you and your potential future love partner can find true happiness in your love relationship/marriage. But if you are already in a relationship or marriage with a love partner who is not sexually compatible with you, then nothing much can be done to fix the problem.

There are number of reasons why men as well as women cheat

in a committed relationship/marriage. For cheating men, sex is the primary motivating factor. For cheating women, the key factors are marital dissatisfaction, ignored, underappreciated, and/or unmet emotional needs. In my opinion Lack of intimacy is one of the main reasons for cheating. You have a nice luxury house, a good job/business on the outside. But inside, the relationship is lacking one important thing that is intimacy. Sex and Intimacy make both love partners connected in a love relationship/marriage for very, very long time. Well women want to feel wanted. If you are not making her feel that way, she could seek it elsewhere if she is not getting it at home. Many times people are unhappy in their relationship or marriage, and break up is difficult and painful. An affair is the easy way out or at least that's how people see it. Women are more likely to have an affair because of loneliness and unmet emotional needs. Men are more likely to go for infidelity for sexual motivations. Of course, the reasons above are not the only reasons why married men and women cheat on their mates. There are other reasons as well. But these are the reasons most frequently cited in by cheating husbands and cheating wives who participated in studies on why men and women cheat.

    Please remember if the ruling planets in your astrology chart (your ascendant sign lord and ascendant nakshatra lord in particular) at the time of your birth have a strong connection with the 5th house in your lover's astrology chart, then your lover can not cheat on you in your relationship because your ruling planets are activating the 5th house of love and sex in your lover's chart. We also had discussed in the previous chapter, that 6th house, 8th house, 12th house and Badhaka house are detrimental to Relationship Compatibility. If your ascendant sign lord and ascendant nakshatra lord have connection with the 6th house or 8th house or 12th house or Badhaka house in your love partner's astrology chart, then the chances are your love partner will cheat on you because of sexual dissatisfaction and lack of intimacy. Your love partner will end up having a love affair with a third person, whose ruling planets (ascendant sign lord and ascendant nakshatra lord) in their astrology chart will have connection with the 5th house or the 7th house in your love partner's astrology chart. Your love partner at that time will be going through the Mahadasha / Bhukti of planets connected with their 5th house of love and sex and / or 7th house of relationships. This is usually a good time for love life and sex.

On the flip side you will end up having a love affair with a third person if your love partner's ruling planets (the ascendant sign lord and ascendant nakshatra lord) at the time of their birth are connected with the 6th house or 8th house or 12th house or badhaka house in your astrology chart. In this scenario you will end up having a love affair with a third person, whose ruling planets (ascendant sign lord and ascendant nakshatra lord) are connected with your 5th house and / or 7th house in your astrology chart. You will find this third person sexually compatible and very intimate. This affair will take place when you will be going through the mahadasha / bhukti of planets connected with the 5th house and / or 7th house in your astrology chart.

It is always good to have more planets connected with the 5th house in your astrology chart, and find a love partner whose ruling planets are activating 5th house in your astrology chart and vice versa, for a complete satisfaction in both partner's love life. This is the best case scenario for happiness in love relationship / marriage. I have seen such cases only 5% of the time in my career as a Professional astrologer. But if you have too many planets in your astrology chart connected with the 4th house (negate sex), 6th house (divorce, separation), 8th house (disappointment, arguments, fights), 12th house (loss of marriage/relationship, loss of money), and Badhaka house (violence, obstacles) in your astrology chart then your astrology chart is not good for love relationship or marriage. In this case you will face disappointment in your love life, may go through divorce/separation, and your life will be a lonely one. I see such configurations in the astrology charts of single and lonely people. Many times they never had any love relationship in their life time, they face disappointment in their love life or they could be in a sexless relationship or marriage.

One should never have a love relationship with a love partner whose ruling planets (the ascendant sign lord and ascendant nakshatra lord) at the time of their birth are connected with the 6th house or 8th house or 12th house or badhaka house in your astrology chart or vice versa. If there is 6th house connection then it is bad for relationship / marriage because 6th house negates 7th house matters. If there is 8th house connection then you both will be arguing and fighting with each other most of the time in a relationship / marriage. If there is 12th house connection then they will be your hidden enemy and will bring financial loss to you. If there is a Badhaka house connection then it can lead to violence in a love relationship or marriage.

Please remember if a planet is evil in your astrology chart or connected with the evil houses as described above, then you will suffer in life due to a person in your life, represented by that planet. The planet is not going to come down from sky to harm you because it is evil in your astrology chart. The planet will send someone in your life, may be a love partner represented by that evil planet, and you suffer in life due to that love partner, because the love partner's ruling planets at the time of their birth, are connected with an evil house in your astrology chart. You will have serious problems with this love partner (represented by evil planets in your astrology chart) when you will be going through the mahadasha / bhukti of such evil planets in your astrology chart. If you are stuck with a wrong person in your love relationship or marriage, any therapy or doctor's advice will not help you much. In the same manner if a planet is good for intimacy and sexual satisfaction in your astrology chart because of 5th house connection, a love partner represented by that planet can make you happy in your love life, and give you full sexual satisfaction, intimacy, and happiness. You can meet such sexually compatible love partner when you are going through the mahadasha / bhukti of the planets connected with the 5th house in your astrology chart. This is my research work in the field of relationship compatibility astrology. I have tested these astrology rules during my relationship compatibility astrology readings and they work for, both straight and gay couples. You will not find this information in any other astrology book or any astrology system available to you. In my opinion, majority of the people end up in a love relationship and marriage with incompatible love partner, because either they got into a love relationship or marriage at wrong time in their life or for wrong reasons. In this case the love partner's ruling planets (ascendant sign lord and ascendant nakshatra lord) are connected with the evil houses in their astrology chart, and they are frustrated and miserable in their personal life. But if you follow the astrology techniques I presented in this book, you are careful in selecting your potential future love partner, I am sure you can find happiness, intimacy and sexual satisfaction in your love relationship and marriage.

We will do couple of case studies to illustrate the type of person that will cheat in a relationship, and why. Why the relationship may end in a separation or divorce. I am using the same two astrology charts that I used in the 'Sexual Compatibility' chapter previously.

CASE STUDY 1

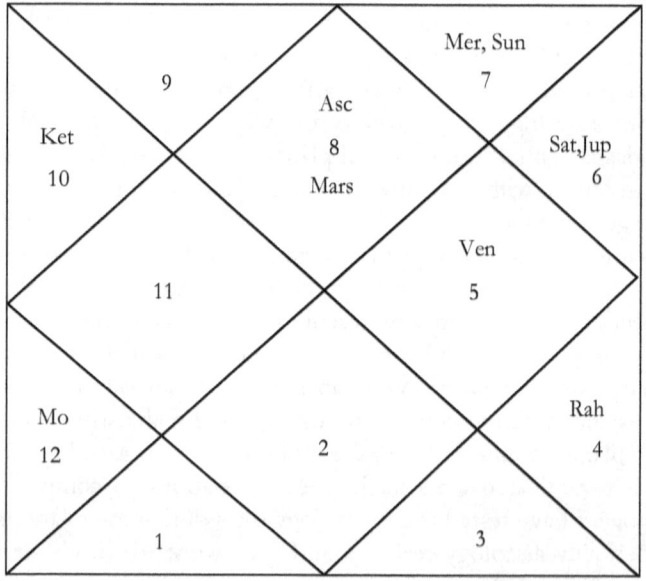

This person is a Scorpio ascendant with ascendant degree at 15 degrees and 22 minutes in Scorpio sign. For Scorpio ascendant, Mars rules the 6th house, and in this astrology chart the 10th house lord Sun is in Mars nakshatra chitra in Libra sign, and Mars is in 12th house. Mercury rules the 8th house and Rahu is in Mercury's nakshatra Aslesha in Cancer sign represented by Badhaka planet Moon. Venus rules the 12th house and is in its own nakshatra P Phalguni in Leo sign. Moon, rules badhaka house, Rahu is in Moon sign, Saturn and Ketu are in Moon's nakshatra. So the planets representing 6th house are Sun and Mars, 8th house are Mercury and Rahu, 12th house are Venus, and Badhaka house are Moon, Rahu, Saturn and Ketu. The final list of planets is: Sun, Mars, Mercury, Rahu, Moon Saturn, Ketu, Venus (Libra sign only). These planets represent the following ascendants:

Aries sign, Cancer sign, Gemini sign (0 degrees to 20 degrees), Libra sign (0 degrees to 20 degrees), Capricorn sign, Aquarius sign (0 degrees to 20 degrees).

So if this person represented by Scorpio ascendant ends up in a love relationship with a love partner whose ruling planets (Ascendant sign lord and nakshatra lord) at the time of their birth are represented by the Aries sign or Cancer sign or Gemini sign (0 degrees to 20 degrees) or Libra sign (0 degrees to 20 degrees) or Capricorn sign or Aquarius sign (0 degrees to 20 degrees) then they will be frustrated and miserable in their love relationship or marriage, and will have a tendency to cheat, and go for a extramarital love affair with a third person whose ruling planets at the time of their birth are activating the 5th house or the 7th house in the Scorpio ascendant's astrology chart. This third person's ascendant according to their astrology chart will fall in Pisces sign, or Sagittarius sign ruled by Jupiter or Taurus ruled by Venus. This Scorpio ascendant will find intimacy and sexual compatibility with this third person with whom they will have a love affair. Now you understand why people cheat in their love relationship and marriage.

GURMEET SINGH

PLANET	LONGITUDE	NAKSHATRA
ASCENDANT	15 Sc 22' 01.30"	ANURADHA
SUN	4 Li 59' 11.68"	CHITRA
MOON	4 Pi 25' 38.93"	U BHADRAPAD
MARS	13 Sc 18' 13.86"	ANURADHA
MERCURY	26 Li 19' 03.43"	VISHAKA
JUPITER	5 Vi 23' 04.76"	U PHALGUNI
VENUS	26 Le 06' 15.36"	P PHALGUNI
SATURN(R)	10 Vi 12' 18.84"	HASTA
RAHU	22 Cn 47' 56.96"	ASLESHA
KETU	22 Cp 47' 56.96"	SHRAVANA

House	Cusp	Middle	End	Planets in it
1ST	15 Sc 22' 01.30"	1 Sg 18' 50.97"	17 Sg 15' 40.65"	ASC
2ND	17 Sg 15' 40.65"	5 Cp 13' 15.20"	23 Cp 10' 49.75"	KETU
3RD	23 Cp 10' 49.75"	10 Aq 55' 49.91"	28 Aq 40' 50.07"	
4TH	28 Aq 40' 50.07"	13 Pi 50' 59.45"	29 Pi 01' 08.84"	MOON
5TH	29 Pi 01' 08.84"	11 Ar 25' 32.03"	23 Ar 49' 55.21"	

RELATIONSHIP COMPATIBILITY ASTROLOGY

6TH	23 Ar 49' 55.21"	4 Ta 35' 58.25"	15 Ta 22' 01.30"	
7TH	15 Ta 22' 01.30"	1 Ge 18' 50.97"	17 Ge 15' 40.65"	
8TH	17 Ge 15' 40.65"	5 Cn 13' 15.20"	23 Cn 10' 49.75"	RAHU
9TH	23 Cn 10' 49.75"	10 Le 55' 49.91"	28 Le 40' 50.07"	VENUS
10TH	28 Le 40' 50.07"	13 Vi 50' 59.45"	29 Vi 01' 08.84"	JUP, SAT
11TH	29 Vi 01' 08.84"	11 Li 25' 32.03"	23 Li 49' 55.21"	SUN
12TH	23 Li 49' 55.21"	4 Sc 35' 58.25"	15 Sc 22' 01.30"	MER, MARS

CASE STUDY 2

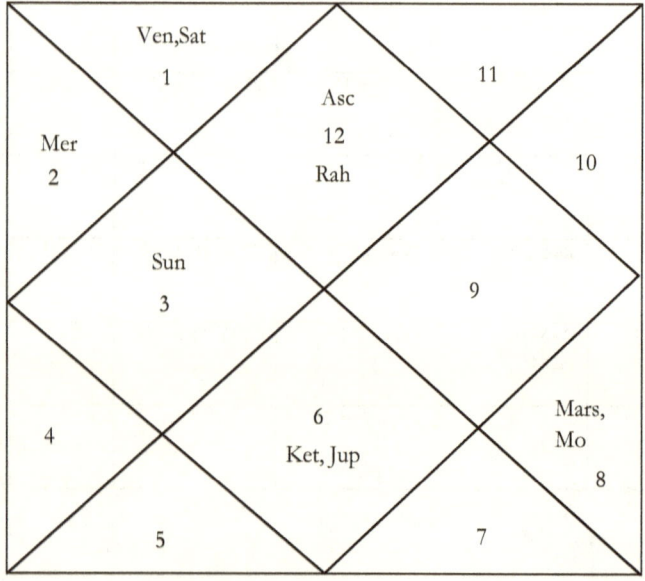

This person is a Pisces ascendant according to Vedic Astrology, with ascendant degree at 22 degrees 47 minutes in Pisces sign ruled by Jupiter. For Pisces ascendant, Sun rules the 6th house. Jupiter and Ketu are in Sun's nakshatra U. Phalguni in Virgo sign, 8th house lord Venus is also in Sun's nakshatra Krittika in Aries sign. Mercury is the Badhaka planet and Ketu is in Mercury's sign, and Saturn rules the 12th house. So the planets representing 6th house are Sun, Jupiter, Venus, Ketu, 8th house are Venus and 12th house are Saturn, Moon, and Mars. We omit Mercury and Moon from this list, because they are connected with the 5th house. The final list of planets is: Sun, Jupiter, Ketu, Venus, and Saturn (Aquarius only). These planets represent the following ascendants:

Aries sign, Leo sign, Libra sign, Aquarius sign.

So if this person represented by Pisces ascendant ends up in a love relationship with a love partner whose ruling planets (Ascendant sign lord and nakshatra lord) at the time of their birth are represented by the Aries sign or Leo sign or Libra sign or Aquarius sign then they will be frustrated and miserable in their

RELATIONSHIP COMPATIBILITY ASTROLOGY

love relationship or marriage, and will have a tendency to cheat, and go for a extramarital love affair with a third person whose ruling planets at the time of their birth are activating the 5th house or the 7th house in the Pisces ascendant's astrology chart. This third person's ascendant according to their astrology chart will fall in Cancer sign (16.40 degrees to 30 degrees) Moon sign Mercury nakshatra, or Virgo sign (10 degrees to 23.20 degrees) Mercury sign Moon nakshatra. This Pisces ascendant will find intimacy and sexual compatibility with this third person with whom they will have a love affair.

PLANET	LONGITUDE	NAKSHATRA
ASCENDANT	22 Pi 47' 07.47"	REVATI
SUN	12 Ge 44' 51.21"	ARDRA
MOON	14 Sc 49' 14.17"	ANURADHA
MARS	11 Sc 17' 29.23"	ANURADHA
MERCURY	22 Ta 59' 29.80"	ROHINI
JUPITER	4 Vi 41' 05.75"	U PHALGUNI
VENUS	29 Ar 23' 11.71"	KRITTIKA
SATURN(R)	13 Ar 29' 27.89"	BHARANI
RAHU	1 Pi 50' 35.61"	P BHADRAPAD
KETU	1 Vi 50' 35.61"	U PHALGUNI

GURMEET SINGH

House	Cusp	Middle	End	Planets in it
1ST	22 Pi 47' 07.47"	10 Ar 04' 25.27"	27 Ar 21' 43.07"	SAT
2ND	27 Ar 21' 43.07"	10 Ta 29' 28.48"	23 Ta 37' 13.90"	VENUS, MER
3RD	23 Ta 37' 13.90"	5 Ge 19' 14.60"	17 Ge 01' 15.29"	SUN
4TH	17 Ge 01' 15.29"	29 Ge 26' 15.82"	11 Cn 51' 16.35"	
5TH	11 Cn 51' 16.35"	27 Cn 13' 50.43"	12 Le 36' 24.52"	
6TH	12 Le 36' 24.52"	2 Vi 41' 46.00"	22 Vi 47' 07.47"	JUP, KET
7TH	22 Vi 47' 07.47"	10 Li 04' 25.27"	27 Li 21' 43.07"	
8TH	27 Li 21' 43.07"	10 Sc 29' 28.48"	23 Sc 37' 13.90"	MOON, MARS
9TH	23 Sc 37' 13.90"	5 Sg 19' 14.60"	17 Sg 01' 15.29"	
10TH	17 Sg 01' 15.29"	29 Sg 26' 15.82"	11 Cp 51' 16.35"	
11TH	11 Cp 51' 16.35"	27 Cp 13' 50.43"	12 Aq 36' 24.52"	
12TH	12 Aq 36' 24.52"	2 Pi 41' 46.00"	22 Pi 47' 07.47"	RAH

5 GAY, LESBIAN TENDENCIES IN THE ASTROLOGY CHART

In this chapter we will discuss how you can find out Gay, Lesbian tendencies in your potential partner. I have been contacted by people for relationship issues, after being in a serious relationship or marriage for quite some time they found out that their partner has Gay or Lesbian tendencies. I have also been contacted by single people with Gay or Lesbian tendencies looking for the right Gay Partner. They are deeply in love with one of their friends, but don't know how to approach their friend, because they are not sure if their friend also has Gay or Lesbian tendencies. By using the divine power of astrology, one can find out from the astrology chart if the person has Gay or Lesbian tendencies, and help them avoid any complications in their relationship matters.

Again the relationship compatibility astrology predictions you read in magazines, and internet sites where the astrologers/psychics are analyzing Zodiac Signs to find out the Gay or Lesbian tendencies in a person do not work in real life, because billions of people around the world are born in a particular month and they could all relate to a particular zodiac sign but they all cannot have Gay or Lesbian tendencies. Even people born in a particular month or on a particular day having same zodiac sign could be completely different in their personality, nature and habits. Then how can you predict Gay or Lesbian tendencies just using the zodiac signs. I also see many Vedic Astrologers using Ketu, Mercury, and Saturn conjunction to predict Gay or Lesbian tendencies in the astrology chart, and that doesn't work either.

The 5th house and 7th house in any astrology chart are the houses of intimacy. 5th house in the astrology chart represents a person's sex life and love affairs. The 7th house in the astrology chart represents relationship matters and the private parts of the individual. When the 5th and 7th house lords in the astrology chart have connection with the 6th house and Badhaka house, by aspect, nakshatras, and close conjunctions, and the mahadasha / bhukti at the time of birth is also of these planets, then the person will have Gay, Lesbian or Bi-sexual tendencies. If the person has gone through the mahadasha and Bhukti of such planets at the time of their birth, then they will be born as Gay or Lesbian. Otherwise when they will go through the mahadasha and bhukti of these planets later in life, they will realize that they are Gay or Lesbian or Bi-sexual. This is the Golden Rule that I have found out from the decades of my research work in the astrology field, and it works.

The following case studies illustrate Gay or Lesbian tendencies, when these astrological configurations of 5th house and 7th house lords with the Badhaka house and 6th house existed in the natal astrology charts of the individuals.

ROCK HUDSON

Rock Hudson was an American actor, widely known as a leading man in the 1950s and 1960s. Hudson is also recognized for dramatic roles in films such as Giant and Magnificent Obsession. In later years, he found success in television, starring in the popular mystery series *McMillan & Wife* and the soap opera Dynasty. Hudson was voted Star of the Year, Favorite Leading Man, and similar titles by numerous film magazines. Hudson, secretly gay for much of his life, died in 1985, becoming the first major celebrity to die from an AIDS-related illness.

Date: November 17, 1925
Time: 2:15:00
Time Zone: 6:00:00 (West of GMT)
Place: 87 W 44' 09", 42 N 06' 29"
Winnetka, Illinois, USA
Ayanamsa: 22-43-30.92
Sidereal Time: 6:07:33

RELATIONSHIP COMPATIBILITY ASTROLOGY

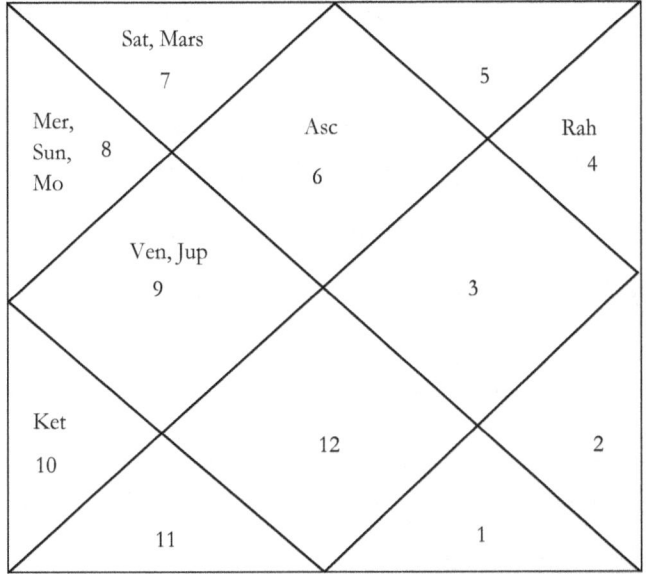

Rock Hudson (born November 17, 1925 at 2:15 AM in Winnetka, Illinois) was a Virgo ascendant, ruled by Mercury, with ascendant degree at 8 degrees 45 minutes in Virgo sign. Jupiter, the lord of 7th house of relationships in the astrology chart, is also the Badhaka Planet for Hudson. Saturn rules the 5th house of sex and love life, also rules the 6th house of sickness and diseases. The 7th house of relationships lord Jupiter is in the Uttarashadha nakshatra, ruled by 12th house lord Sun, and Jupiter is very closely aspected by 5th house and 6th house lord Saturn. The 5th and 6th house lord Saturn is in the Vishakha nakshatra ruled by Badhaka lord, and 7th house lord Jupiter. The close connection of 5th, 6th, and Badhaka (7th) lord in the Rock Hudson's astrology chart clearly indicates homosexual tendencies. Since Hudosn was born in Saturn Mahadasha Jupiter Bhukti, so he was born as a Gay person. Natal Moon in Rock Hudson's astrology chart is in 5th and 6th house lord Saturn's Anuradha nakshatra, and Badhaka Planet Jupiter's sub. It was during Moon Mahdasha (June 1977 to June 1987), Hudson was diagnosed with HIV on June 5th, 1984. On October 2, 1985, in Moon mahadasha Venus Bhukti, Hudson died in his sleep from AIDS-related complications at his home in Beverly Hills

GURMEET SINGH

PLANET	LONGITUDE	NAKSHATRA
ASCENDANT	8 Vi 45' 04.31"	U. PHALGUNI
SUN	1 Sc 45' 27.14"	VISHAKA
MOON	15 Sc 34' 18.66"	ANURADHA
MARS	9 Li 47' 29.87"	SWATI
MERCURY	22 Sc 59' 35.61"	JYESHTA
JUPITER	26 Sg 48' 10.09"	UTTARASHADHA
VENUS	18 Sg 37' 30.60"	PURVASHADHA
SATURN(R)	25 Li 11' 07.26"	VISHAKA
RAHU	5 Cn 56' 45.65"	PUSHYAMI
KETU	5 Cp 56' 45.65"	UTTARASHADHA

House	Cusp	Middle	End	Planets in it
1ST	8 Vi 45' 04.31"	21 Vi 42' 32.68"	4 Li 40' 01.04"	ASC
2ND	4 Li 40' 01.04"	19 Li 54' 02.12"	5 Sc 08' 03.19"	SUN, MARS, SAT
3RD	5 Sc 08' 03.19"	22 Sc 04' 10.05"	9 Sg 00' 16.90"	MOON, MER
4TH	9 Sg 00' 16.90"	25 Sg 54' 11.43"	12 Cp 48' 05.97"	JUP, VEN, KETU
5TH	12 Cp 48'	27 Cp 56' 50.32"	13 Aq 05' 34.68"	

		05.97"			
6TH	13 Aq 05' 34.68"	25 Aq 55' 19.49"	8 Pi 45' 04.31"		
7TH	8 Pi 45' 04.31"	21 Pi 42' 32.68"	4 Ar 40' 01.04"		
8TH	4 Ar 40' 01.04"	19 Ar 54' 02.12"	5 Ta 08' 03.19"		
9TH	5 Ta 08' 03.19"	22 Ta 04' 10.05"	9 Ge 00' 16.90"		
10TH	9 Ge 00' 16.90"	25 Ge 54' 11.43"	12 Cn 48' 05.97"	RAHU	
11TH	12 Cn 48' 05.97"	27 Cn 56' 50.32"	13 Le 05' 34.68"		
12TH	13 Le 05' 34.68"	25 Le 55' 19.49"	8 Vi 45' 04.31"		

Vimsottari Dasa:
Maha Dasas:
    Sat: 1908-06-06 - 1927-06-07
    Merc: 1927-06-07 - 1944-06-07
    Ket: 1944-06-07 - 1951-06-07
    Ven: 1951-06-07 - 1971-06-07
    Sun: 1971-06-07 - 1977-06-07
    Moon: 1977-06-07 - 1987-06-08
    Mars: 1987-06-08 - 1994-06-07
    Rah: 1994-06-07 - 2012-06-07
    Jup: 2012-06-07 - 2028-06-07

RACHEL MADDOW:

Rachel Anne Maddow (born April 1, 1973 at 12:23 PM in Hayward California) is an American television host, political commentator, and author. She hosts a nightly television show, The Rachel Maddow Show, on MSNBC. Maddow is the first openly gay anchor to host a major prime-time news program in the United States.

Date: April 1, 1973
Time: 12:23:00
Time Zone: 8:00:00 (West of GMT)
Place: 120 W 22' 13", 37 N 38' 34"
                Hayward, California, USA
Ayanamsa: 23-23-12.75
Sidereal Time: 1:01:43

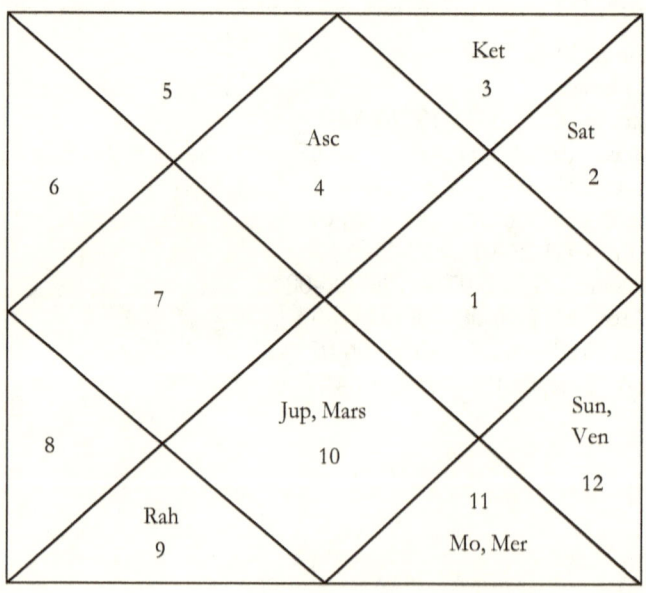

According to Vedic Astrology, Maddow is a Cancer ascendant ruled by Moon with ascendant degree at 6 degrees 21 minutes in Cancer sign. Since the ascendant is in the beginning of the Cancer sign, the 11th house (Badhaka for Cancer ascendant) cusp lies at 29

degrees 25 minutes in Aries, ruled by Mars. Mercury rules the 12th house. Saturn rules the 7th house of relationships and 8th house of loss. Jupiter rules the 6th house. We can understand the lesbian tendencies in the Maddow's astrology chart by analyzing the 7th house lord Saturn and the 5th house lord Venus (5th house cusp stays in Libra sign). In the natal astrology chart, the 7th house lord Saturn is in the Badhaka house (11th house) in Taurus sign, and it is aspected by the 6th house lord Jupiter from Capricorn sign, in the 7th house of relationships. We see that the 7th house of relationships lord is connected with the Badhaka house and the 6th house, clearly indicates lesbian tendencies in the astrology chart. If we analyze the 5th house lord Venus, she is in the nakshatra of Saturn and Saturn again is aspected by the 6th house lord Jupiter. The 5th house lord is again connected with the 6th house. The mahadasha at the time of birth is again Jupiter, ruler of the 6th house, activated the lesbian tendencies at the time of birth.

PLANET	LONGITUDE	NAKSHATRA
ASCENDANT	6 Cn 21' 43.74"	PUSHYAMI
SUN	18 Pi 34' 51.49"	REVATI
MOON	27 Aq 05' 10.10"	P BHADRAPAD
MARS	10 Cp 51' 18.91"	SHRAVANA
MERCURY	22 Aq 58' 17.40"	P BHADRAPAD
JUPITER	13 Cp 40' 52.61"	SHRAVANA
VENUS	16 Pi 33' 03.99"	U BHADRAPAD
SATURN(R)	22 Ta 14' 55.35"	ROHINI
RAHU	19 Sg 03' 02.00"	PURVASHADHA
KETU	19 Ge 03' 02.00"	ARDRA

GURMEET SINGH

House	Cusp	Middle	End	Planets in it
1ST	6 Cn 21' 43.74"	16 Cn 51' 42.85"	27 Cn 21' 41.96"	ASC
2ND	27 Cn 21' 41.96"	9 Le 51' 36.60"	22 Le 21' 31.24"	
3RD	22 Le 21' 31.24"	7 Vi 51' 24.54"	23 Vi 21' 17.83"	
4TH	23 Vi 21' 17.83"	11 Li 23' 18.67"	29 Li 25' 19.51"	
5TH	29 Li 25' 19.51"	17 Sc 18' 23.73"	5 Sg 11' 27.96"	
6TH	5 Sg 11' 27.96"	20 Sg 46' 35.85"	6 Cp 21' 43.74"	RAHU
7TH	6 Cp 21' 43.74"	16 Cp 51' 42.85"	27 Cp 21' 41.96"	MARS, JUP
8TH	27 Cp 21' 41.96"	9 Aq 51' 36.60"	22 Aq 21' 31.24"	
9TH	22 Aq 21' 31.24"	7 Pi 51' 24.54"	23 Pi 21' 17.83"	SUN, MOON, MER, VENUS
10TH	23 Pi 21' 17.83"	11 Ar 23' 18.67"	29 Ar 25' 19.51"	
11TH	29 Ar 25' 19.51"	17 Ta 18' 23.73"	5 Ge 11' 27.96"	SAT
12TH	5 Ge 11' 27.96"	20 Ge 46' 35.85"	6 Cn 21' 43.74"	KETU

Vimsottari Dasa:
Maha Dasas:
   Jup: 1964-10-03 - 1980-10-03
   Sat: 1980-10-03 - 1999-10-04
   Merc: 1999-10-04 - 2016-10-03
   Ket: 2016-10-03 - 2023-10-04
   Ven: 2023-10-04 - 2043-10-04
   Sun: 2043-10-04 - 2049-10-04
   Moon: 2049-10-04 - 2059-10-04
   Mars: 2059-10-04 - 2066-10-04
   Rah: 2066-10-04 - 2084-10-04

RICKY MARTIN

Enrique "Ricky" Martín Morales (born December 24, 1971), is a Puerto Rican pop musician, actor and author. His first English-language album (also titled *Ricky Martin*), has sold 22 million copies and is one of the best selling albums of all time. On March 29, 2010, Martin publicly acknowledged his homosexuality in a post on his official website stating, "I am proud to say that I am a fortunate homosexual man. I am very blessed to be who I am. Martin said that "these years in silence and reflection made me stronger and reminded me that acceptance has to come from within, and that this kind of truth gives me the power to conquer emotions I didn't even know existed.

   Date: December 24, 1971
   Time: 17:00:00
   Time Zone: 4:00:00 (West of GMT)
   Place: 66 W 03' 00", 18 N 25' 00"
   Ayanamsa: 23-22-08.88
   Sidereal Time: 22:46:44

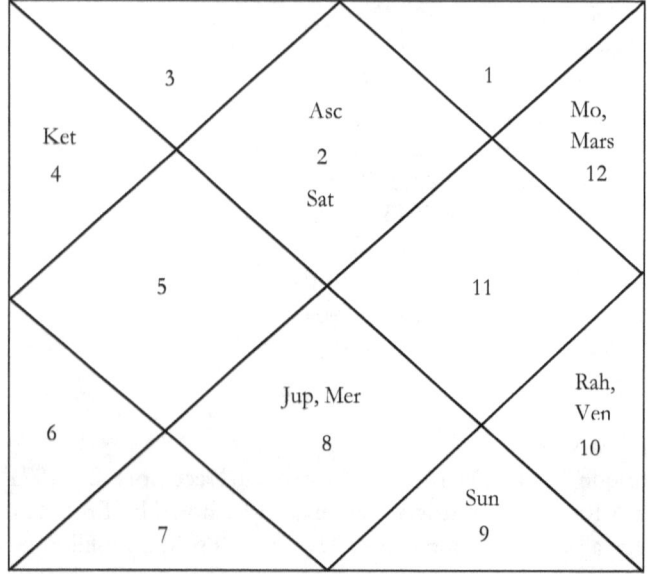

Ricky Martin born on December 24th, 1971 at 5:00 PM in Hato Rey, Puerto Rico is a Taurus ascendant, ruled by Venus and the ascendant degree is 27 degrees 18 minutes in Taurus sign. Now by analyzing the 5th house (sex) lord and the 7th house (relationships) lord, we can find out the homosexual tendencies in the Ricky Martin's astrology chart. For Taurus ascendant, the three evil lords are Saturn, Mars, and Jupiter. Saturn rules the badhaka (9th) house, Mars rules the evil 12th house, and Jupiter rules the evil 8th house. The 7th house of relationships lord Mars also rules the 12th house, and is positioned in the 10th house in the natal astrology chart, in 8th house lord Jupiter's Pisces sign, and badhaka planet Saturn's Uttarabhadhra nakshatra. Also the 8th house lord Jupiter from Scorpio aspects natal Mars in Pisces. The 5th house lord Mercury is in 6th house, as Mercury is before the 7th house cusp, and Mercury is again aspected by the Badhaka Planet Saturn in the astrology chart. This clearly indicates homosexual tendencies in the Ricky Martin's astrology chart. Martin publicly acknowledged his homosexuality during Ketu Mahadasha Mercury Bhukti (June 2009 to May 2010).

RELATIONSHIP COMPATIBILITY ASTROLOGY

PLANET	LONGITUDE	NAKSHATRA
ASCENDANT	27 Ta 18' 27.86"	MRIGASHIRA
SUN	9 Sg 02' 08.53"	MOOLA
MOON	6 Pi 32' 18.51"	U BHADRAPAD
MARS	5 Pi 25' 38.62"	U BHADRAPAD
MERCURY	18 Sc 53' 59.68"	JYESHTA
JUPITER	27 Sc 23' 39.36"	JYESHTA
VENUS	8 Cp 37' 16.31"	UTTARASHADHA
SATURN(R)	7 Ta 27' 50.74"	KRITTIKA
RAHU	13 Cp 38' 15.00"	SHRAVANA
KETU	13 Cn 38' 15.00"	PUSHYAMI

House	Cusp	Middle	End	Planets in it
1ST	27 Ta 18' 27.86"	9 Ge 47' 30.98"	22 Ge 16' 34.10"	ASC
2ND	22 Ge 16' 34.10"	5 Cn 03' 54.40"	17 Cn 51' 14.70"	KETU
3RD	17 Cn 51' 14.70"	2 Le 19' 18.52"	16 Le 47' 22.34"	
4TH	16 Le 47' 22.34"	3 Vi 22' 40.01"	19 Vi 57' 57.68"	
5TH	19 Vi 57' 57.68"	7 Li 20' 45.91"	24 Li 43' 34.14"	

6TH	24 Li 43' 34.14"	11 Sc 01' 01.00"	27 Sc 18' 27.86"	MER
7TH	27 Sc 18' 27.86"	9 Sg 47' 30.98"	22 Sg 16' 34.10"	SUN. JUP
8TH	22 Sg 16' 34.10"	5 Cp 03' 54.40"	17 Cp 51' 14.70"	VENUS, RAHU
9TH	17 Cp 51' 14.70"	2 Aq 19' 18.52"	16 Aq 47' 22.34"	
10TH	16 Aq 47' 22.34"	3 Pi 22' 40.01"	19 Pi 57' 57.68"	MOON, MARS
11TH	19 Pi 57' 57.68"	7 Ar 20' 45.91"	24 Ar 43' 34.14"	
12TH	24 Ar 43' 34.14"	11 Ta 01' 01.00"	27 Ta 18' 27.86"	SAT

Vimsottari Dasa:
Maha Dasas:
Sat: 1967-05-30 - 1986-05-29
Merc: 1986-05-29 - 2003-05-30
Ket: 2003-05-30 - 2010-05-30
Ven: 2010-05-30 - 2030-05-30
Sun: 2030-05-30 - 2036-05-29
Moon: 2036-05-29 - 2046-05-30
Mars: 2046-05-30 - 2053-05-30
Rah: 2053-05-30 - 2071-05-30
Jup: 2071-05-30 - 2087-05-30

ANDERSON COOPER:

Anderson Hays Cooper (born June 3, 1967 at 3:46 PM in New York, NY) is an American journalist, author and television personality. He is the primary anchor of the CNN news show Anderson Cooper 360. Cooper also served as host of his own eponymous syndicated daytime talk show Anderson Live. Cooper is openly gay, according to The New York Times. He is the most prominent openly gay journalist on American television. For years, Cooper avoided discussing his private life in interviews. On July 2nd, 2012 Cooper publicly stated that he is gay, always have been, always will be.

Date: June 3, 1967
Time: 15:46:00
Time Zone: 4:00:00 (West of GMT)
Place: 74 W 00' 23", 40 N 42' 51"
            New York, New York, USA
Ayanamsa: 23-18-19.65
Sidereal Time: 7:36:16

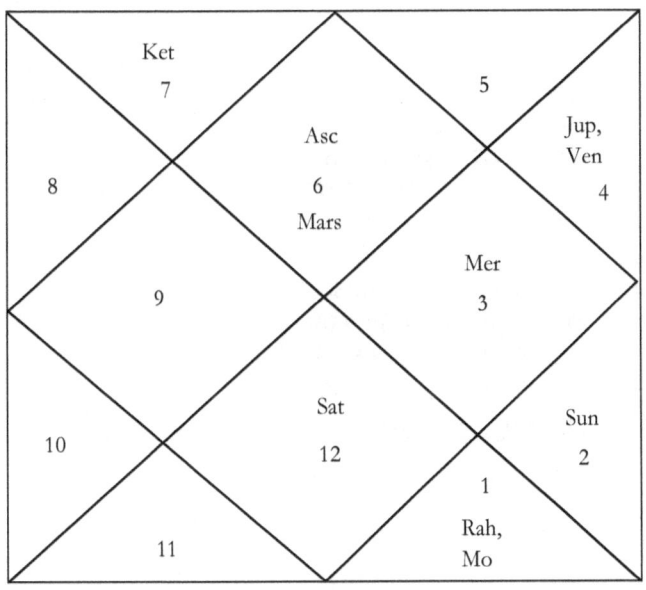

Here I have an interesting story to share with my readers. In the summer of 2010, one of my close friends, wanted to discuss Anderson Cooper's astrology chart with me, as she had crush on Anderson Cooper. I analyzed Anderson Cooper's natal astrology chart, and scheduled the reading with my friend. I mentioned to her at that time, that Cooper may not be interested in women because according to his astrology chart, Cooper has gay tendencies. She couldn't believe me at that time. I gave her a call almost two years later, when Cooper publicly admitted that he is gay. She was shocked at the accuracy of my reading, and wanted to learn astrology.

Anderson Cooper is a Virgo ascendant, ruled by Mercury, with ascendant degree at 25 degrees 45 minutes in Virgo sign. The 7th house (relationships) lord Jupiter also rules 6th house in the astrology chart as the 6th house cusp stays in Pisces sign. Jupiter is a Badhaka planet for Virgo ascendant. Natal Jupiter is in Cancer sign in the Pushyami nakshatra ruled by 5th house lord Saturn and Saturn is in 6th house. The 5th house lord Saturn is in Pisces sign, aspected by the Badhaka planet Jupiter, by its 9th aspect. The connection of the 5th house lord, 6th house lord and the Badhaka house lord (7th) clearly indicates the gay tendencies in the Cooper's astrology chart.

Vimsottari Dasa:
Maha Dasas:
Ket: 1967-05-07 - 1974-05-07
Ven: 1974-05-07 - 1994-05-07
Sun: 1994-05-07 - 2000-05-07
Moon: 2000-05-07 - 2010-05-07
Mars: 2010-05-07 - 2017-05-07
Rah: 2017-05-07 - 2035-05-08
Jup: 2035-05-08 - 2051-05-08
Sat: 2051-05-08 - 2070-05-08
Merc: 2070-05-08 - 2087-05-08

RELATIONSHIP COMPATIBILITY ASTROLOGY

PLANET	LONGITUDE	NAKSHATRA
ASCENDANT	25 Vi 45' 29.52"	CHITRA
SUN	19 Ta 14' 08.06"	ROHINI
MOON	0 Ar 08' 11.38"	ASWINI
MARS	22 Vi 07' 40.65"	HASTA
MERCURY	11 Ge 20' 23.74"	ARDRA
JUPITER	8 Cn 38' 25.39"	PUSHYAMI
VENUS	3 Cn 41' 19.57"	PUSHYAMI
SATURN(R)	17 Pi 01' 43.09"	REVATI
RAHU	11 Ar 52' 19.12"	ASWINI
KETU	11 Li 52' 19.12"	SWATI

House	Cusp	Middle	End	Planets in it
1ST	25 Vi 45' 29.52"	9 Li 28' 52.20"	23 Li 12' 14.89"	ASC, KETU
2ND	23 Li 12' 14.89"	8 Sc 57' 04.95"	24 Sc 41' 55.02"	
3RD	24 Sc 41' 55.02"	11 Sg 50' 14.52"	28 Sg 58' 34.03"	
4TH	28 Sg 58' 34.03"	15 Cp 38' 41.10"	2 Aq 18' 48.18"	
5TH	2 Aq 18' 48.18"	16 Aq 54' 55.03"	1 Pi 31' 01.89"	

6TH	1 Pi 31' 01.89"	13 Pi 38' 15.70"	25 Pi 45' 29.52"	SAT
7TH	25 Pi 45' 29.52"	9 Ar 28' 52.20"	23 Ar 12' 14.89"	MOON, RAHU
8TH	23 Ar 12' 14.89"	8 Ta 57' 04.95"	24 Ta 41' 55.02"	SUN
9TH	24 Ta 41' 55.02"	11 Ge 50' 14.52"	28 Ge 58' 34.03"	MER
10TH	28 Ge 58' 34.03"	15 Cn 38' 41.10"	2 Le 18' 48.18"	JUP, VENUS
11TH	2 Le 18' 48.18"	16 Le 54' 55.03"	1 Vi 31' 01.89"	
12TH	1 Vi 31' 01.89"	13 Vi 38' 15.70"	25 Vi 45' 29.52"	MARS

CHAZ BONO:

Chaz Salvatore Bono – (born Chastity Sun Bono, March 4, 1969 at 0:55 AM, Concord California) is an American advocate, writer, and musician. He is the only child of American entertainers Sonny and Cher, though each had children from other relationships. Chaz is a transgender man. In 1995, Bono publicly self-identified as such in a cover story in a leading American gay monthly magazine. Between 2008 and 2010, Bono underwent female-to-male gender transition.

Date: March 4, 1969
Time: 0:55:00
Time Zone: 8:00:00 (West of GMT)
Place: 122 W 01' 48", 37 N 58' 41"
        Concord, California, USA
Ayanamsa: 23-19-47.69
Sidereal Time: 11:34:40

RELATIONSHIP COMPATIBILITY ASTROLOGY

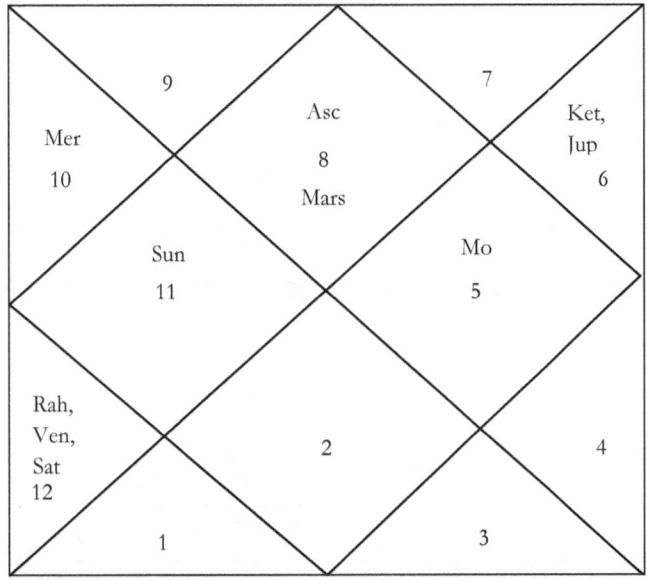

Bono is a Scorpio ascendant ruled by Mars. The ascendant degree is at 14 degrees 9 minutes in Scorpio sign. In his case by analyzing the ascendant lord Mars and planets connected with Mars, we will understand why Bono is a transgender man, and went through female-to-male gender transition. For Scorpio Mars rules the 1st house (self) and the 6th house (health issues). In Bono's case Mars is in 12th house, as it lies before the ascendant degree in Scorpio sign. The Planet Mercury, ruler of 8th house (surgery) and 11th house (cure) is in Mars Dhanistha nakshatra in Capricorn sign in the natal astrology chart. Mercury connects 1st house (self), 6th house (health issues), 12th house (hospitalization), 8th house (surgery), and 11th house (cure). Mercury is a dual planet, In 1995 when Bono publicly self identified in a cover story in a leading American gay monthly magazine, Bono was going through Mars Mahadasha, Mercury Bhukti. Bono was in Rahu mahadasha Mercury Bhukti in 2008 and 2009, when Bono underwent female-to-male gender transition. Mercury, a dual planet played an important role during female-to-male gender transition surgery.

GURMEET SINGH

PLANET	LONGITUDE	NAKSHATRA
ASCENDANT	14 Sc 09' 42.89"	ANURADHA
SUN	20 Aq 17' 17.39"	P BHADRAPAD
MOON	22 Le 05' 43.28"	P PHALGUNI
MARS	9 Sc 47' 59.84"	ANURADHA
MERCURY	25 Cp 02' 48.87"	DHANISHTA
JUPITER	10 Vi 00' 28.37"	HASTA
VENUS	29 Pi 52' 48.76"	REVATI
SATURN(R)	29 Pi 46' 13.32"	REVATI
RAHU	7 Pi 58' 51.69"	U BHADRAPAD
KETU	7 Vi 58' 51.69"	U PHALGUNI

House	Cusp	Middle	End	Planets in it
1ST	14 Sc 09' 42.89"	0 Sg 20' 17.78"	16 Sg 30' 52.67"	ASC
2ND	16 Sg 30' 52.67"	5 Cp 04' 41.25"	23 Cp 38' 29.83"	
3RD	23 Cp 38' 29.83"	11 Aq 42' 20.99"	29 Aq 46' 12.15"	SUN, MER
4TH	29 Aq 46' 12.15"	14 Pi 44' 12.91"	29 Pi 42' 13.66"	RAHU
5TH	29 Pi 42' 13.66"	11 Ar 40' 33.88"	23 Ar 38' 54.11"	VENUS, SAT

RELATIONSHIP COMPATIBILITY ASTROLOGY

6TH	23 Ar 38' 54.11"	3 Ta 54' 18.50"	14 Ta 09' 42.89"	
7TH	14 Ta 09' 42.89"	0 Ge 20' 17.78"	16 Ge 30' 52.67"	
8TH	16 Ge 30' 52.67"	5 Cn 04' 41.25"	23 Cn 38' 29.83"	
9TH	23 Cn 38' 29.83"	11 Le 42' 20.99"	29 Le 46' 12.15"	MOON
10TH	29 Le 46' 12.15"	14 Vi 44' 12.91"	29 Vi 42' 13.66"	KETU, JUP
11TH	29 Vi 42' 13.66"	11 Li 40' 33.88"	23 Li 38' 54.11"	
12TH	23 Li 38' 54.11"	3 Sc 54' 18.50"	14 Sc 09' 42.89"	MARS

Vimsottari Dasa:
Maha Dasas:
   Ven: 1956-01-12 - 1976-01-12
   Sun: 1976-01-12 - 1982-01-12
   Moon: 1982-01-12 - 1992-01-13
   Mars: 1992-01-13 - 1999-01-12
     Antardasas in this MD:
     Mars: 1992-01-13 - 1992-06-09
     Rah: 1992-06-09 - 1993-06-28
     Jup: 1993-06-28 - 1994-06-03
     Sat: 1994-06-03 - 1995-07-15
     Merc: 1995-07-15 - 1996-07-11
     Ket: 1996-07-11 - 1996-12-07
     Ven: 1996-12-07 - 1998-02-05
     Sun: 1998-02-05 - 1998-06-13
     Moon: 1998-06-13 - 1999-01-12
   Rah: 1999-01-12 - 2017-01-12
     Antardasas in this MD:
     Rah: 1999-01-12 - 2001-09-27
     Jup: 2001-09-27 - 2004-02-17
     Sat: 2004-02-17 - 2006-12-26

Merc: 2006-12-26 - 2009-07-14
Ket: 2009-07-14 - 2010-08-02
Ven: 2010-08-02 - 2013-08-02
Sun: 2013-08-02 - 2014-06-26
Moon: 2014-06-26 - 2015-12-26
Mars: 2015-12-26 - 2017-01-12
Jup: 2017-01-12 - 2033-01-12
Sat: 2033-01-12 - 2052-01-13
Merc: 2052-01-13 - 2069-01-12
Ket: 2069-01-12 - 2076-01-13

6 LONGEVITY AND HEALTH OF SPOUSE

Good Health and longevity is important for Relationship Compatibility and Marriage. Most definitely you want to be in relationship with a love partner who has good health and long life. A healthy body allows for a healthy sex life. Good Health is the foundation of a long term loving relationship. In my work with gay, lesbian and straight couples, the issue of health and longevity comes up frequently. This is because good health and longevity matters in Love Relationships. More frequently my clients ask questions such as, 'Is my love partner going to have good health and longevity?', 'Am I going to have good health and longevity in my lifetime?', 'How can I assess good health and longevity of a potential future partner?', 'When the health issues will come up in my life or my love partner's life?' Marriages or love relationships sometimes cannot survive if the couples do not have good health and longevity. In other words Health and Longevity is a deal breaker in some love relationships and marriages. Medical Astrology is the branch of the Astrology that deals with Health and Longevity issues. Each sign and each planet are associated with a number of possible diseases. So it may be said that the native may be affected by such disease or diseases. In my opinion the function of the astrologer ends with saying that the particular part of the body will be sensitive to acute or chronic disease. Only the medical doctor alone is competent authority to name the disease.

The 6th house denotes the sickness, 8th house surgery, death, and 12th house hospitalization. Disease is indicated by 6, danger by 8 and defect by 12. If the sub lord of 12th cusp is in 6, the house of disease, and if the sub lord is in the constellation of the planet occupying or owning 6 or 8 or 12 it is definite that one will have the defect from the time when the significators conjointly operate. If the sub lord of the ascendant is in the constellation of the significator of 6 or 8 or 12 then one suffers from disease or danger or hospitalization. The following houses represent health issues in the astrology chart:

SIXTH HOUSE: Sixth house in the astrology chart is known as the 'house of sicknesses'. It indicates disease and sickness. The health will break down only when one runs the mahadashas or Bhuktis of planets connected with the 6th house. Planets in any manner connected to the 6th house have to cause disease. Hence in their conjoined periods they produce such results. Any planet can own the 6th house or occupy the constellation or sub of lord of 6. Therefore all planets are capable of causing ailment.

EIGHTH HOUSE: Eighth house in the astrology chart is considered to have direct bearing upon one's longevity or span of life in this world. It is necessary to consider 1st and 3rd house also in addition to the 8th house for longevity. The 8th house is called the 'house of death', the end of life in this world. Eighth house has to do with misfortune, mental anxiety, accident, surgery, suicide, and danger from disease.

TWELFTH HOUSE: Twelfth house in the astrology chart is the house of hospitalization, confinement, imprisonment, loss by marriage, loss of wife, loss of any kind, expenses, donations, charity work, secret enemies, deception, and repayment of loan.

For cure, consider the 1st, 5th, and 11th. 1st - health, 5th is 12th to the 6th - or absence of sickness, 11th is 12th to 12 - or absence of bedridden sickness. Whenever one suffers from any disease, one will be running the period of the planet connected with 6th house. He can expect cure during the sub period of the planet connected with ascendant or 5th house or 11th house. A Virgo born will be sick when they run the period of a planet in Scorpio, in Saturn star, and sun sub. The following houses represent cure from disease or good health in the astrology chart:

FIRST HOUSE: First house or the Ascendant is always an important house when it comes to the health of the native. It also indicates native's physical stature, vitality and vigor. If the ascendant cusp lord and the ascendant lord are well placed by house, nakshatras, aspect and conjunction, it gives good health to the native.

FIFTH HOUSE: Fifth house is the house of cure or absence of sickness as it is 12th house to the 6th house of sickness and disease. In other words, 5th house negate 6th house matters, that is sickness and disease. During the period of the planets connected with the 5th house, the health of the native improves, and they find cure if they have any health issues.

ELEVENTH HOUSE: Planets in any manner connected with 11th house cure disease as 11th is the 6th to the 6th. No person can have a cure from the chronic disease, if there is no planet in the 11th house, no planet in the constellation of the owner or occupant of 11th house and if the 11th cusp and the lord of the 11th are in the sub of evil planets. Horoscopes of sick people reveal that the lords of the dasas which they experienced they contracted disease are all in the sub of lord of 6, and the 11th house is not strong. Lord of 11 and 1 are also spoiled. 11th house which is 12th to the 12th house governs discharge from the hospital.

AFFLICTIONS IN SIGNS: Each sign and each planet are associated with a number of possible diseases. Planets in movable signs cause disease of short duration; Common signs indicate neither short nor long. Fixed signs threaten disease of prolonging, chronic, and tedious nature. If planets are afflicted in movable or cardinal signs they affect head, stomach, kidneys and skin. Diseases, for example, brain fever, epilepsy, sudden unconsciousness (apoplexy); stomach trouble, cancer; kidney and liver troubles; rheumatism, gout and colds or chills. Afflictions in fixed signs affect throat, heart, urine-genital organs and blood. Diseases, for example, tonsillitis, diphtheria, heart troubles, spinal ailments, piles, stones, ailments regarding urinary and generative organs; blood disorders. Afflictions in common or mutable signs affect lungs, intestines, nerves and digestion. It represents diseases, for example, TB, bronchitis, asthma, intestinal diseases, rheumatism; dropsy, scurvy.

SIGNS AND PARTS OF THE BODY:

Aries: Head, brain, face
Taurus: Throat, neck, lips, ears
Gemini: Lungs, hands, arms, shoulders
Cancer: Stomach, breasts, chest, digestive organs, ribs, elbows
Leo: Heart, back, spine, wrists, forearms.
Virgo: Intestines, lower spine, fingers, abdomen, spleen
Libra: Kidneys, skin, lumbar region
Scorpio: Urinary and generative organs, bladder, anus, pelvis, nose, appendix
Sagittarius: Hips, thighs, nerves, arteries
Capricorn: Knees, joints, bones, teeth, skin
Aquarius: Legs, ankles, circulation of blood
Pisces: Feet, toes, lymphatic system

PLANETS AND ORGANS OF THE BODY:

Sun: Heart, back, spleen, blood, brain, right eye of a man, left eye of a woman, vitality
Moon: Stomach, uterus, ovaries, breasts, saliva, left eye of a man, right eye of a woman
Mercury: Nerves, mind, brain, tongue, speech, lungs, hands, arms, ears, hair
Venus: Throat, internal generative organs, kidneys, ovaries, complexion, reins, veins, cheeks
Mars: External generative organs, rectum, Nose, forehead, gall bladder, muscles, bile
Jupiter: Liver, arteries, hip bones, feet, thighs, arteries, right ear
Saturn: Bones, gall bladder, skin, left ear, joints, teeth, spleen,

SIGNIFICATORS OF HEALTH:

Ascendant: The degree rising on the cusp of the Ascendant is of great importance in judging the health. It rules the body. The bodily strength and its power of resisting disease may be judged from the Ascendant. Health suffers when the sub lord of the ascendant is in the constellation of the significator of 6 or 8 or 12. If the sub lord of the Ascendant is in the star of the occupant of the 1st or the 11th, the health is normal. f the sub lord of the ascendant is in the star of the occupant or owner of the 6th (disease and sickness), the 8th (danger to life), or the 12th (bedridden illness), this is not good for matters of health.

Sun: It rules the vitality, constitution of the body.

Moon: It rules the functional system of the body. It is of primary importance in the case of a child. It is a very important significator of health in the chart of a woman.

Sixth House: It is a house of sickness, ailments and diseases. Disease is judged from the sign on the cusp of the 6th house, planets in the 6th house, ruler of the 6th house, and planets connected with the 6th house.

Thus Sun, Moon, Ascendant, the ruler of the Ascendant, the ruler of the 6th house, planets in the 6th house, and planets connected with the 6th house are the significators of health. Saturn when afflicted in the astrology chart causes diseases for want of proper nourishment, chronic and lingering ailments, dislocations, sprains, falls, blows, rheumatism, colds, chills, bruises. Mars when afflicted in the astrology chart causes sharp and sudden diseases, accidents, surgeries, fevers, inflammatory diseases. Jupiter when afflicted in the astrology chart causes liver trouble, gout, blood disorder, ailments arising from excessive eating and indiscretion in diet. Mental instability or madness is judged from the afflictions to moon and mercury by the malefics. Mercury rules speech and hearing. If sun and moon are afflicted, eyes are weak. Mars denotes operations, sharp and sudden diseases. Saturn lingering diseases like gangrene, paralysis.

The following celebrity case studies illustrate such health issues, when the malefic astrological configurations described above, converge in the natal horoscopes of the individuals

ROBIN ROBERTS

Robin René Roberts (born November 23, 1960, 10:30 AM, Pass Christian, Mississippi) is an American television broadcaster. Roberts is the anchor of ABC's morning show *Good Morning America*. Roberts was a sportscaster on ESPN for 15 years (1990–2005). She became co-anchor on *Good Morning America* in 2005. She has been treated for breast cancer and for myelodysplastic syndrome. Robin has a long time girl friend for 10 years.

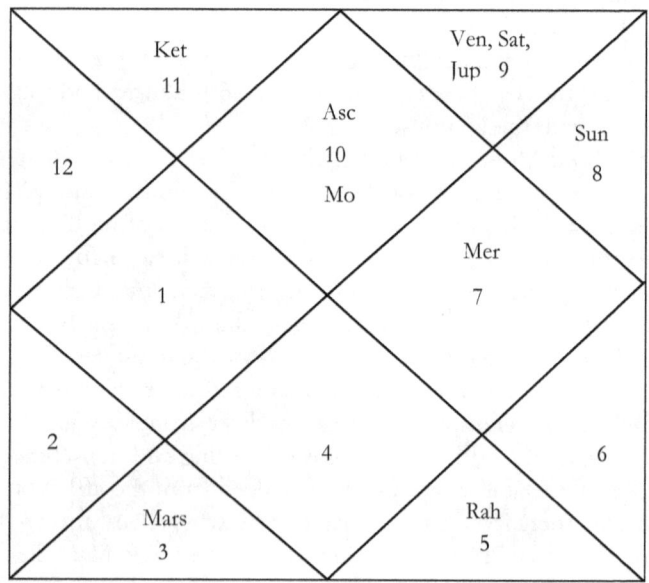

Robin is a Capricorn Ascendant, ruled by Saturn with the ascendant degree at 2 degrees 44 minutes in Capricorn sign. For Capricorn ascendant Mars, the ruler of 11th house and 4th house is a Badhaka planet. In Robin's astrology chart Mars in positioned in 6th house of diseases and sickness. Mars from its position in 6th house of sicknesses, and diseases, is aspecting the ascendant lord Saturn's natal position in 12th house. Mars is in 12th house and 3rd house lord Jupiter's constellation Punarvasu in Gemini sign, and is directly aspected by the 12th house (hospitalization) lord Jupiter.

This planetary configuration is not good for Robin's health. During Jupiter mahadasha Mars Bhukti in 2007, Roberts was diagnosed with an early form of breast cancer. She underwent surgery on August 3 2007, and by January 2008 had completed eight chemotherapy treatments, followed by six and a half weeks of radiation treatment. Mars from 6th house is also aspecting the natal position of Moon in the first house, by its 8th aspect, gave Robin Breast Cancer at that time. As moon represents Breasts for women, according to the Planets and Organs of the body list provided at the beginning of this chapter. The 7th house lord Moon (relationships) is in 1st house in Capricorn sign and in its own nakshatra Shravana. Moon is aspected by Badhaka Planet Mars from its position in 6th house, by its 8th aspect. In other words the 7th house lord Moon is connected with the Badhaka planet Mars and with 6th house as well, because Mars is in 6th house and aspects Moon. This is the reason for lesbian sexual orientation in Robin's case.

Robin was in Saturn Mahadasha and Saturn Bhukti in 2012, when she was diagnosed with myelodysplastic syndrome (MDS), a disease of the bone marrow. Saturn during 2012 was transiting Chitra nakshatra ruled by badhaka planet Mars in Virgo and Libra signs. Robin got a bone marrow transplant in 2013 during Saturn mahadasha and 6th house lord Mercury Bhukti. The ascendant and Mahadasha lord Saturn was afflicted by Rahu due to Saturn Rahu conjunction in 2013.

GURMEET SINGH

PLANET	LONGITUDE	NAKSHATRA
ASCENDANT	2 Cp 44' 44.47"	UTTARASHADHA
SUN	8 Sc 11' 30.68"	ANURADHA
MOON	12 Cp 27' 20.75"	SHRAVANA
MARS	25 Ge 22' 45.20"	PURNAVASU
MERCURY	18 Li 27' 55.28"	SWATI
JUPITER	12 Sg 17' 28.45"	MOOLA
VENUS	16 Sg 50' 33.68"	PURVASHADHA
SATURN(R)	22 Sg 12' 13.09"	PURVASHADHA
RAHU	18 Le 09' 33.27"	P PHALGUNI
KETU	18 Aq 09' 33.27"	SHATABISHA

House	Cusp	Middle	End	Planets in it
1ST	2 Cp 44' 44.47"	22 Cp 25' 02.69"	12 Aq 05' 20.91"	ASC, MOON
2ND	12 Aq 05' 20.91"	0 Pi 54' 06.41"	19 Pi 42' 51.91"	KETU
3RD	19 Pi 42' 51.91"	4 Ar 55' 29.33"	20 Ar 08' 06.75"	
4TH	20 Ar 08' 06.75"	2 Ta 32' 48.82"	14 Ta 57' 30.90"	
5TH	14 Ta 57' 30.90"	26 Ta 22' 45.47"	7 Ge 48' 00.05"	

6TH	7 Ge 48' 00.05"	20 Ge 16' 22.26"	2 Cn 44' 44.47"	MARS
7TH	2 Cn 44' 44.47"	22 Cn 25' 02.69"	12 Le 05' 20.91"	
8TH	12 Le 05' 20.91"	0 Vi 54' 06.41"	19 Vi 42' 51.91"	RAHU
9TH	19 Vi 42' 51.91"	4 Li 55' 29.33"	20 Li 08' 06.75"	MER
10TH	20 Li 08' 06.75"	2 Sc 32' 48.82"	14 Sc 57' 30.90"	SUN
11TH	14 Sc 57' 30.90"	26 Sc 22' 45.47"	7 Sg 48' 00.05"	
12TH	7 Sg 48' 00.05"	20 Sg 16' 22.26"	2 Cp 44' 44.47"	JUP, VEN, SAT

STEVE JOBS

Steven Jobs (born February 24, 1955, rectified birth time 18:49 PM San Francisco CA), was the co-founder and chief executive officer of Apple Inc. Jobs died at his Palo Alto, California, home around 3 pm on October 5, 2011, due to complications from a relapse of his previously treated islet-cell neuroendocrine pancreatic cancer resulting in respiratory arrest.

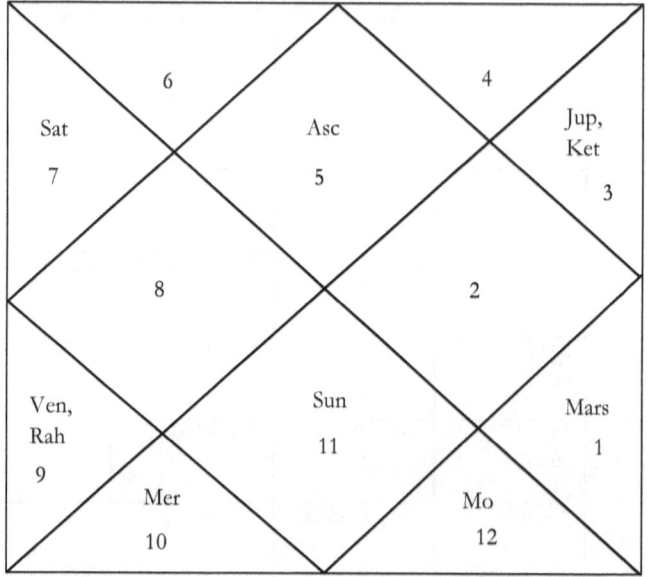

Disease is judged from the sign on the cusp of the 6th house, planets in the 6th house. Planets in any manner connected to the 6th house have to cause disease. Hence in their conjoined periods they produce the results. Steve Jobs is a Leo Ascendant, and the lord of 6th houses of diseases is Saturn. Saturn causes diseases for want of proper nourishment, chronic and lingering ailments, rheumatism, cancer, colds, chills, dull aches, pancreatic cancer, falls, blows, sprains, dislocations, bruises, Bones, joints, teeth, spleen, gall bladder, skin, left ear.

Steve Jobs achieved a very high level of success during Ketu period (1975 to 1982), then Venus period (1982 to 2002) and finally sun period (2002 to 2008). Ketu is very strong in 11th house in Mercury's sign. Venus rules the 10th house of career, and 3rd house of change, that is why during the Venus period there were too many changes in Jobs career. In Steve Jobs astrology chart Moon rules the 12th house of hospitalization and is located in 8th house of surgery, and is in the constellation of 6th house of sickness lord Saturn, and Saturn is in 3rd of change. The Nakshatra lord Saturn is directly aspected by the badhaka planet Mars. In October 2003, Jobs was diagnosed with cancer when Jobs was going through Sun mahadasha and Rahu bhukti in his astrology chart. Rahu is also evil for health as it is aspected by the 6th house lord Saturn. In my opinion the health problem started sometime in 2002 during Sun mahadasha Moon bhukti, but was diagnosed later in 2003.

Moon mahadasha 2008 onwards, activated the 6th house of sickness, 8th house of surgery, and 12th house of hospitalization in Steve Jobs astrology chart, and the transit Saturn from Virgo was directly aspecting the 12th house lord Moon's natal position. 6th, 8th and 12th houses when activated through Mahadasha and Bhukti always bring health issues, loss of money and decline in career/fortune. Transit Saturn during year 2011 was directly opposite the natal position of Moon in Steve Jobs astrology chart. Jobs died on October 5th, 2011 during Moon mahadasha Jupiter bhukti (8th house lord).

PLANET	LONGITUDE	NAKSHATRA
ASCENDANT	23 Le 51' 06.70"	P PHALGUNI
SUN	12 Aq 35' 47.63"	SHATABISHA
MOON	14 Pi 21' 08.82"	U BHADRAPAD
MARS	5 Ar 56' 46.37"	ASWINI
MERCURY	21 Cp 13' 22.94"	SHRAVANA
JUPITER	27 Ge 22' 05.82"	PURNAVASU
VENUS	28 Sg 01' 05.24"	UTTARASHADHA
SATURN(R)	28 Li 01' 25.55"	VISHAKA
RAHU	9 Sg 22' 00.43"	MOOLA
KETU	9 Ge 22' 00.43"	ARDRA

GURMEET SINGH

House	Cusp	Middle	End	Planets in it
1ST	23 Le 51' 06.70"	6 Vi 35' 48.99"	19 Vi 20' 31.28"	ASC
2ND	19 Vi 20' 31.28"	4 Li 16' 02.76"	19 Li 11' 34.24"	
3RD	19 Li 11' 34.24"	5 Sc 40' 26.40"	22 Sc 09' 18.55"	SAT
4TH	22 Sc 09' 18.55"	8 Sg 49' 05.76"	25 Sg 28' 52.97"	RAHU
5TH	25 Sg 28' 52.97"	10 Cp 57' 40.62"	26 Cp 26' 28.28"	MER, VENUS
6TH	26 Cp 26' 28.28"	10 Aq 08' 47.49"	23 Aq 51' 06.70"	SUN
7TH	23 Aq 51' 06.70"	6 Pi 35' 48.99"	19 Pi 20' 31.28"	MOON
8TH	19 Pi 20' 31.28"	4 Ar 16' 02.76"	19 Ar 11' 34.24"	MARS
9TH	19 Ar 11' 34.24"	5 Ta 40' 26.40"	22 Ta 09' 18.55"	
10TH	22 Ta 09' 18.55"	8 Ge 49' 05.76"	25 Ge 28' 52.97"	KETU
11TH	25 Ge 28' 52.97"	10 Cn 57' 40.62"	26 Cn 26' 28.28"	JUP
12TH	26 Cn 26' 28.28"	10 Le 08' 47.49"	23 Le 51' 06.70"	

RELATIONSHIP COMPATIBILITY ASTROLOGY

BLADE RUNNER OSCAR PISTARIUS

Oscar Leonard Carl Pistorius born 22 November 1986 at 10:18 AM in Sandton, South Africa) is a South African sprint runner. Although both of Pistorius' legs were amputated below the knee when he was 11 months old, he competes in events for single below-knee amputees and for able-bodied athletes. On 14 February 2013, Pistorius was charged with the murder of his girlfriend Reeva Steenkamp, whom he had fatally shot at his home in the early hours of that morning. He was granted bail on 22 February 2013 and at a subsequent hearing on 19 August 2013 dates were set for a trial from 3 to 20 March 2014.

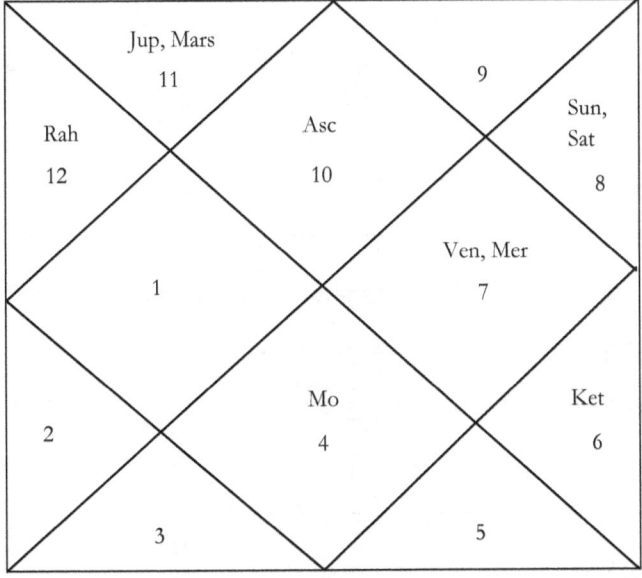

Oscar Pistorius is a Capricorn ascendant with ascendant degree at 16 degrees 34 minutes in Capricorn sign. For Capricorn ascendant the 11th house ruled by Mars is the Badhaka house. Scorpio sign falls in the 11th house. The ascendant Lord Saturn is positioned in Scorpio sign in 11th house (Badhaka house), very close to 11th house cusp and in 6th house lord Mercury's Jyestha nakshatra. Oscar Pistorius was born in Saturn mahadasha as Moon at the time of birth is in Pushyami nakshatra ruled by Saturn, in Cancer sign. 11th house represents legs, and in this astrology chart the ascendant lord Saturn is in 11th house, in Badhaka house and 6th house lord Mercury's nakshatra. This was the main reason why both of Pistorius's legs were amputated below the knee when he was only 11 months old. Saturn rules Capricorn sign and Aquarius sign. Capricorn sign represents knees and Aquarius sign represents legs. Pistorius was in Saturn Mahadasha and Sun the ruler of 8th house lord's Bhukti when the legs were amputated.

PLANET	LONGITUDE	NAKSHATRA
ASCENDANT	16 Cp 34' 00.62"	SHRAVANA
SUN	6 Sc 09' 32.72"	ANURADHA
MOON	9 Cn 51' 05.41"	PUSHYAMI
MARS	3 Aq 54' 00.02"	DHANISTA
MERCURY	19 Li 30' 34.88"	SWATI
JUPITER	19 Aq 43' 30.70"	SHATABHISHA
VENUS	11 Li 36' 41.60"	SWATI
SATURN(R)	17 Sc 10' 52.79"	JYESTHA
RAHU	25 Pi 01' 04.54"	REVATI
KETU	25 Vi 01' 04.54"	CHITRA

RELATIONSHIP COMPATIBILITY ASTROLOGY

House	Cusp	Middle	End	Planets in it
1ST	16 Cp 34' 00.62"	28 Cp 58' 19.20"	11 Aq 22' 37.79"	ASC, MARS
2ND	11 Aq 22' 37.79"	25 Aq 43' 43.50"	10 Pi 04' 49.21"	JUP
3RD	10 Pi 04' 49.21"	26 Pi 12' 14.39"	12 Ar 19' 39.57"	RAHU
4TH	12 Ar 19' 39.57"	28 Ar 54' 24.91"	15 Ta 29' 10.25"	
5TH	15 Ta 29' 10.25"	1 Ge 17' 15.63"	17 Ge 05' 21.02"	
6TH	17 Ge 05' 21.02"	1 Cn 49' 40.82"	16 Cn 34' 00.62"	MOON
7TH	16 Cn 34' 00.62"	28 Cn 58' 19.20"	11 Le 22' 37.79"	
8TH	11 Le 22' 37.79"	25 Le 43' 43.50"	10 Vi 04' 49.21"	
9TH	10 Vi 04' 49.21"	26 Vi 12' 14.39"	12 Li 19' 39.57"	VENUS, KETU
10TH	12 Li 19' 39.57"	28 Li 54' 24.91"	15 Sc 29' 10.25"	SUN, MER
11TH	15 Sc 29' 10.25"	1 Sg 17' 15.63"	17 Sg 05' 21.02"	SAT
12TH	17 Sg 05' 21.02"	1 Cp 49' 40.82"	16 Cp 34' 00.62"	

ARTHUR ASHE

Arthur Robert Ashe, Jr. (born July 10, 1943, at 12:55PM Richmond, Virginia) was an American World No. 1 professional tennis player. He won three Grand Slam titles, ranking him among the best tennis players from the United States. Ashe, an African American, was the first black player ever selected to the United States Davis Cup team and the only black man ever to win the singles title at Wimbledon, the US Open, and the Australian Open. In the early 1980s, Ashe contracted HIV from a blood transfusion he received during heart bypass surgery. Ashe publicly announced his illness in April 1992 and began working to educate others about HIV and AIDS. He founded the Arthur Ashe Foundation for the Defeat of AIDS and the Arthur Ashe Institute for Urban Health before his death from AIDS related pneumonia on February 6, 1993.

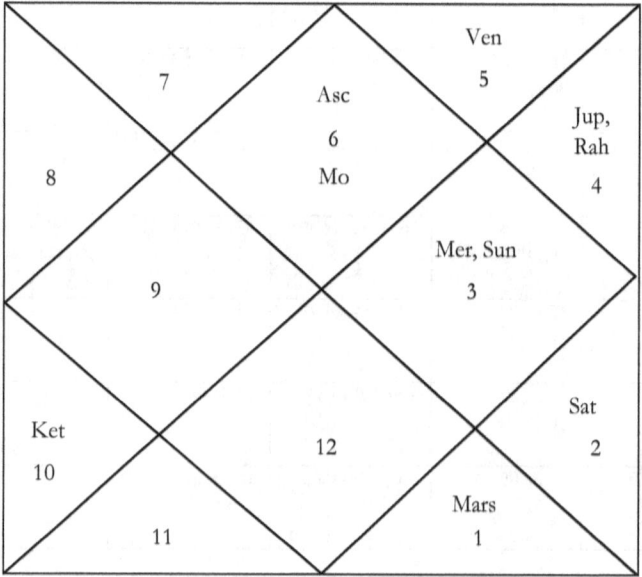

Arthur Ashe is a Virgo ascendant with ascendant degree at 18 degrees 29 minutes in Virgo sign. For Virgo ascendant Saturn rules the 6th house of diseases, Mars rules the 8th house of surgery and longevity, Sun rules the 12th house of hospitalization, and 7th house lord Jupiter is the badhaka planet. The ascendant lord Mercury is in Gemini sign in Ardra nakshatra ruled by Rahu. The nakshatra lord Rahu although positioned in the 11th house is aspected by the 6th house of diseases lord Saturn, 8th house of surgery and longevity lord Mars, and Rahu is in conjunction with the Badhaka planet Jupiter. The ascendant lord Mercury is also in conjunction with the 12th house of hospitalization lord Sun in Gemini sign. So many malefic planets for health are influencing the ascendant lord Mercury, resulted in health issues for Arthur Ashe.

PLANET	LONGITUDE	NAKSHATRA
ASCENDANT	18 Vi 29' 13.65"	HASTA
SUN	24 Ge 35' 25.91"	PURNAVASU
MOON	24 Vi 47' 48.33"	CHITRA
MARS	8 Ar 55' 53.98"	ASWINI
MERCURY	15 Ge 48' 24.48"	ARDRA
JUPITER	9 Cn 09' 17.68"	PUSHYAMI
VENUS	9 Le 21' 04.29"	MAGHA
SATURN(R)	27 Ta 13' 53.92"	MRIGASHIRA
RAHU	24 Cn 26' 45.37"	ASLESHA
KETU	24 Cp 26' 45.37"	DHANISTA

GURMEET SINGH

House	Cusp	Middle	End	Planets in it
1ST	18 Vi 29' 13.65"	2 Li 09' 36.37"	15 Li 49' 59.08"	ASC, MOON
2ND	15 Li 49' 59.08"	1 Sc 16' 25.99"	16 Sc 42' 52.90"	
3RD	16 Sc 42' 52.90"	3 Sg 19' 38.99"	19 Sg 56' 25.07"	
4TH	19 Sg 56' 25.07"	6 Cp 24' 15.37"	22 Cp 52' 05.68"	
5TH	22 Cp 52' 05.68"	7 Aq 50' 25.12"	22 Aq 48' 44.57"	KETU
6TH	22 Aq 48' 44.57"	5 Pi 38' 59.11"	18 Pi 29' 13.65"	
7TH	18 Pi 29' 13.65"	2 Ar 09' 36.37"	15 Ar 49' 59.08"	MARS
8TH	15 Ar 49' 59.08"	1 Ta 16' 25.99"	16 Ta 42' 52.90"	
9TH	16 Ta 42' 52.90"	3 Ge 19' 38.99"	19 Ge 56' 25.07"	MER, SAT
10TH	19 Ge 56' 25.07"	6 Cn 24' 15.37"	22 Cn 52' 05.68"	SUN, JUP
11TH	22 Cn 52' 05.68"	7 Le 50' 25.12"	22 Le 48' 44.57"	VEN, RAHU
12TH	22 Le 48' 44.57"	5 Vi 38' 59.11"	18 Vi 29' 13.65"	

PETER JENNINGS

Peter Charles Archibald Ewart Jennings, (born July 29, 1938, at 5:00 AM, Toronto, Ontario, Canada) was a Canadian American journalist and news anchor. He was the sole anchor of ABC's World News Tonight from 1983 until his death in 2005 of complications from lung cancer. Peter Jennings announced on April 5, 2005 that he had been diagnosed with lung cancer. He died on August 7, 2005 in Manhattan, a little more than a week after his 67th birthday.

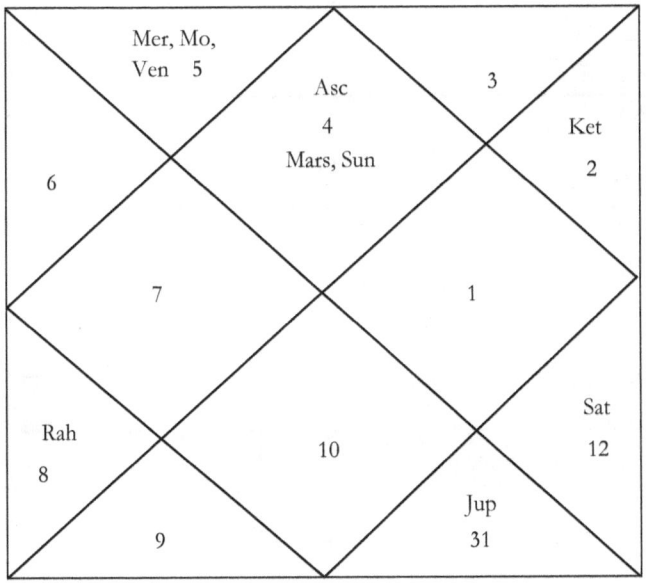

Peter Jennings is a Cancer Ascendant ruled by Moon, the ascendant degree is at 11 degrees 13 minutes in Cancer sign. For Cancer ascendant, Jupiter rules the 6th house of diseases, Saturn rules the 8th house of surgery and longevity, Mercury rules the 12th house of hospitalization, and 11th house lord Venus is the Badhaka planet. Now if we analyze the ascendant lord Moon, we find that Moon is in conjunction with the 12th house lord Mercury, and Badhaka lord Venus. Moon, Mercury, Venus are also aspected by the 6th house of diseases lord Jupiter. This indicates diseases connected with Moon, Mercury, and Venus. Mercury rules lungs, and Peter Jennings died of lung cancer in Jupiter mahadasha and Ketu Bhukti in August 2005. In my opinion Jennings contracted lung cancer during Jupiter mahadasha mercury Bhukti (Nov 2002 to Feb 2005), as Mercury rules lungs.

PLANET	LONGITUDE	NAKSHATRA
ASCENDANT	11 Cn 13' 20.09"	PUSHYAMI
SUN	12 Cn 42' 59.76"	PUSHYAMI
MOON	14 Le 15' 39.51"	P PHALGUNI
MARS	11 Cn 16' 47.94"	PUSHYAMI
MERCURY	9 Le 49' 46.51"	MAGHA
JUPITER	7 Aq 10' 03.05"	SHATABHISHA
VENUS	24 Le 29' 08.45"	P PHALGUNI
SATURN(R)	25 Pi 08' 22.09"	REVATI
RAHU	0 Sc 13' 04.37"	VISHAKA
KETU	0 Ta 13' 04.37"	KRITTIKA

House	Cusp	Middle	End	Planets in it
1ST	11 Cn 13' 20.09"	20 Cn 58' 11.54"	0 Le 43' 02.99"	ASC, SUN, MARS
2ND	0 Le 43' 02.99"	12 Le 41' 58.04"	24 Le 40' 53.09"	MOON, MER,

RELATIONSHIP COMPATIBILITY ASTROLOGY

				VENUS
3RD	24 Le 40' 53.09"	10 Vi 06' 45.32"	25 Vi 32' 37.55"	
4TH	25 Vi 32' 37.55"	14 Li 13' 46.25"	2 Sc 54' 54.95"	RAHU
5TH	2 Sc 54' 54.95"	21 Sc 30' 38.39"	10 Sg 06' 21.83"	
6TH	10 Sg 06' 21.83"	25 Sg 39' 50.96"	11 Cp 13' 20.09"	
7TH	11 Cp 13' 20.09"	20 Cp 58' 11.54"	0 Aq 43' 02.99"	
8TH	0 Aq 43' 02.99"	12 Aq 41' 58.04"	24 Aq 40' 53.09"	JUP
9TH	24 Aq 40' 53.09"	10 Pi 06' 45.32"	25 Pi 32' 37.55"	SAT
10TH	25 Pi 32' 37.55"	14 Ar 13' 46.25"	2 Ta 54' 54.95"	KETU
11TH	2 Ta 54' 54.95"	21 Ta 30' 38.39"	10 Ge 06' 21.83"	
12TH	10 Ge 06' 21.83"	25 Ge 39' 50.96"	11 Cn 13' 20.09"	

7 VIOLENT AND CRIMINAL TENDENCIES IN THE ASTROLOGY CHART

Violent and Criminal Behaviors are unacceptable in any kind of relationship, love or business. In this chapter we will discuss how astrology can help you understand the personality, nature, character, and temperament of your potential spouse before entering into a love or business relationship with them. Obviously one does not want to be in relationship with some abusive, violent and criminal person, with bad temper. One's life is completely shattered when one becomes a victim of cheating in love or business relationships. For example, after getting engaged or married you come to know that the person is already married or have criminal and violent tendencies. After getting into a business partnership with someone, one comes to know the person is manipulating the affairs causing financial loss, and tensions. In Western Astrology the violent and criminal behaviors are judged from the zodiac sign of the individual, which seldom works correctly. I don't know how you could say that one sign is more aligned to criminality than other. Hitler was born in Aries sign, does not mean everyone born in Aries sign is like Hitler. Billions of people around the world are born in a particular month and they could all relate to a particular zodiac sign, could be completely different in their personality, nature and habits. One can learn a lot about their potential partner through an exploration of positions, placements, and aspects in astrology birth (natal) charts. Love and sex are areas of our lives that intrigue us all. There are specific things to look for in the astrology chart that will help shed light on the individual's temperament, personality, character, and nature.

In my opinion, it is not the Zodiac sign of the potential partner, but the ascendant lord, ascendant nakshatra lord, Moon sign lord, and the moon nakshatra lord, and the position of aggressive planet Mars in the astrology chart of the potential partner that tells a lot about the character of the person, whether, the person has criminal tendencies or is a thief or business person or spiritual person. When the ascendant lord or Moon in an astrology chart is connected with the Badhaka house, 8th house & 12th house through constellations (nakshatras), aspects, conjunctions, and is placed in that part of the zodiac ruled by planets which are significators of Badhaka House, 8th house and 12th house, the person will be a violent person, a criminal, a thief, or a killer, and will be very controlling by nature, short tempered, always want things done their way. This person will not be fair to other people in their dealings. The 7th house in the astrology chart is equally important, because the 7th house represents people around you including your potential partner, competitors, enemies etc. If the 7th house lord in your astrology chart is connected with the Badhaka house, 6th house, 8th hours and 12th house through constellations (nakshatras), aspects, conjunctions, and is placed in that part of the zodiac ruled by planets which are significators of Badhaka House, 6th house, 8th house and 12th house, can also result in fights, arguments, and violent behavior in a relationship. The position of violent and aggressive planet Mars in certain houses such as 2nd house, 6th house, 8th house, and 12th house can also result in violence in a relationship. The interpretation of dashas / bhuktis and transits can help one pin point the timing of such acts. When I see such tendencies in my clients astrology charts, I always warn them of eminent danger. One should never rely on such person, and should use extreme caution in having any kind of relationship or friendship with such person. I know that breaking up a committed relationship or marriage is so difficult and painful. But if you are in a relationship or marriage with such abusive and violent person with criminal tendencies according to their astrology chart, then it may be better for you to end such relationship or marriage before any unfortunate incident happens in your life. In my opinion, any kind of therapy or counseling would not make any difference in such a relationship or marriage.

The following case studies illustrate such violent and criminal behaviors, when these malefic astrological configurations of ascendant lord and Moon described above, converge in the natal horoscopes of the individuals.

SCOTT PETERSON:

Scott Peterson was born in San Diego California on October 24, 1972 at 9:36 AM, is a man convicted of murdering his wife Laci Peterson and their unborn son in Modesto California in 2002. Peterson's arrest and subsequent trial received significant American news media coverage until 2005, when he was sentenced to death by lethal injection.

Scott Peterson is Scorpio ascendant ruled by Mars with ascendant degree at 9 degrees 35 minutes in Scorpio sign. If we analyze the ascendant lord Mars in this astrology chart we can understand the personality, character, violent and criminal tendencies in Peterson's case. For Scorpio ascendant, the 9th house lord Moon is the Badhaka (Most Evil) Planet, Mercury rules the evil 8th house and Venus rules the evil 12th house. The ascendant lord Mars represents Scott Peterson, and it rules 1st house and 6th house in his astrology chart. Mars is placed in the 11th house in Virgo sign ruled by 8th house lord Mercury, as Gemini sign falls in 8th house, also ruled by Mercury. Mars in Virgo sign is in the Hastha Nakshatra ruled by Moon, the Badhaka Planet for Scorpio ascendant. The ascendant lord Mars is strongly connected with the 8th house and the Badhaka house, it clearly indicates violent and criminal tendencies in Peterson's case.

The details of Peterson's astrology chart are provided below:

Date: October 24, 1972
Time: 9:36:00
Time Zone: 7:00:00 (West of GMT)
Place: 117 W 09' 23", 32 N 42' 55"
             San Diego, California, USA
KP Ayanamsa: 23-22-50.84
Sidereal Time: 11:00:04

RELATIONSHIP COMPATIBILITY ASTROLOGY

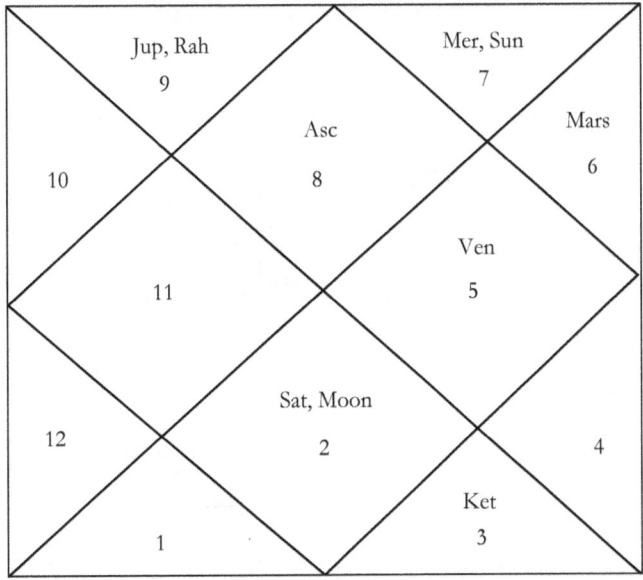

Scott Peterson was in Rahu Mahadasha from August 1990 to August 2008. Rahu is well placed in 2nd house in Jupiter's sign, Sagittarius. Jupiter is the best planet for Scorpio Ascendant as it rules 2nd house of money, and 5th house of love affairs, and sexual pleasures. Rahu in Sagittarius, represents Jupiter, also gave Scott Peterson many love affairs, while he was still married to Laci Peterson. In my opinion the problem in his marriage already started in the beginning of 2002 as mahadasha lord Rahu and Saturn were transiting 7th house in his astrology chart at same time, and there was Rahu and Saturn conjunction that took place in the summer of 2002 in Taurus sign in Peterson's 7th house. Then Saturn's transit through Gemini sign was so bad for Scott Peterson that transit Saturn from Gemini aspected both the mahadasha lord Rahu's natal position in Sagittarius sign by its 7th aspect, and the Bhukti lord Venus's natal position in Leo sign by its 3rd aspect. On March 16th, 2005, Scott Peterson was formally sentenced to death. Saturn at that time was at 26 degrees 35 minutes in Gemini sign directly aspected natal Rahu at 27 degree, 29 minutes in Sagittarius and natal Venus 29 degrees 12 minutes in Leo.

GURMEET SINGH

PLANET	LONGITUDE	NAKSHATRA
ASCENDANT	9 Sc 35' 40.05"	ANURADHA
SUN	7 Li 59' 12.07"	SWATI
MOON	8 Ta 13' 37.74"	KRITTIKA
MARS	22 Vi 00' 48.86"	HASTA
MERCURY	28 Li 44' 49.01"	VISHAKA
JUPITER	10 Sg 21' 10.61"	MOOLA
VENUS	29 Le 12' 09.70"	U. PHALGUNI
SATURN(R)	26 Ta 46' 12.55"	MRIGASHIRA
RAHU	27 Sg 29' 04.71"	UTTARASHADHA
KETU	27 Ge 29' 04.71"	PURNAVASU

House	Cusp	Middle	End	Planets in it
1ST	9 Sc 35' 40.05"	25 Sc 03' 52.19"	10 Sg 32' 04.32"	ASC, JUP
2ND	10 Sg 32' 04.32"	27 Sg 50' 58.09"	15 Cp 09' 51.85"	RAHU
3RD	15 Cp 09' 51.85"	2 Aq 45' 40.76"	20 Aq 21' 29.67"	
4TH	20 Aq 21' 29.67"	5 Pi 57' 26.14"	21 Pi 33' 22.61"	
5TH	21 Pi 33' 22.61"	4 Ar 29' 20.56"	17 Ar 25' 18.51"	

6TH	17 Ar 25' 18.51"	28 Ar 30' 29.28"	9 Ta 35' 40.05"	MOON
7TH	9 Ta 35' 40.05"	25 Ta 03' 52.19"	10 Ge 32' 04.32"	SAT
8TH	10 Ge 32' 04.32"	27 Ge 50' 58.09"	15 Cn 09' 51.85"	KET
9TH	15 Cn 09' 51.85"	2 Le 45' 40.76"	20 Le 21' 29.67"	
10TH	20 Le 21' 29.67"	5 Vi 57' 26.14"	21 Vi 33' 22.61"	VEN
11TH	21 Vi 33' 22.61"	4 Li 29' 20.56"	17 Li 25' 18.51"	SUN, MARS
12TH	17 Li 25' 18.51"	28 Li 30' 29.28"	9 Sc 35' 40.05"	MER

Vimsottari Dasa:
Maha Dasas:

Sun: 1967-08-11 - 1973-08-11
Moon: 1973-08-11 - 1983-08-11
Mars: 1983-08-11 - 1990-08-11
Rah: 1990-08-11 - 2008-08-11
  Antardasas in this MD:
    Rah: 1990-08-11 - 1993-04-20
    Jup: 1993-04-20 - 1995-09-17
    Sat: 1995-09-17 - 1998-07-23
    Merc: 1998-07-23 - 2001-02-07
    Ket: 2001-02-07 - 2002-02-25
    Ven: 2002-02-25 - 2005-02-25
      Pratyantardasas in this AD:
        Ven: 2002-02-25 - 2002-08-30
        Sun: 2002-08-30 - 2002-10-24
        Moon: 2002-10-24 - 2003-01-21
        Mars: 2003-01-21 - 2003-03-24
        Rah: 2003-03-24 - 2003-09-08

                Jup: 2003-09-08 - 2004-01-30
                Sat: 2004-01-30 - 2004-07-23
                Merc: 2004-07-23 - 2004-12-25
                Ket: 2004-12-25 - 2005-02-25
        Sun: 2005-02-25 - 2006-01-20
            Pratyantardasas in this AD:
                Sun: 2005-02-25 - 2005-03-13
                Moon: 2005-03-13 - 2005-04-09
                Mars: 2005-04-09 - 2005-04-29
                Rah: 2005-04-29 - 2005-06-18
                Jup: 2005-06-18 - 2005-08-02
                Sat: 2005-08-02 - 2005-09-24
                Merc: 2005-09-24 - 2005-11-10
                Ket: 2005-11-10 - 2005-11-28
                Ven: 2005-11-28 - 2006-01-20
        Moon: 2006-01-20 - 2007-07-24
        Mars: 2007-07-24 - 2008-08-11
Jup: 2008-08-11 - 2024-08-11
Sat: 2024-08-11 - 2043-08-12
Merc: 2043-08-12 - 2060-08-11
Ket: 2060-08-11 - 2067-08-12
Ven: 2067-08-12 - 2087-08-12

JODI ARIAS:

This chart is of Jodi Arias born on July 9th, 1980 at 1:52 AM in Salinas California. Jodi Arias was charged with murder of her ex boyfriend Travis Alexander, a salesman, was killed at his home in Mesa, Arizona on June 4th, 2008. Her trail began on January 2nd, 2013. Arias testified that she killed Alexander in self defense. She was found guilty of first degree murder on May 8th, 2013.

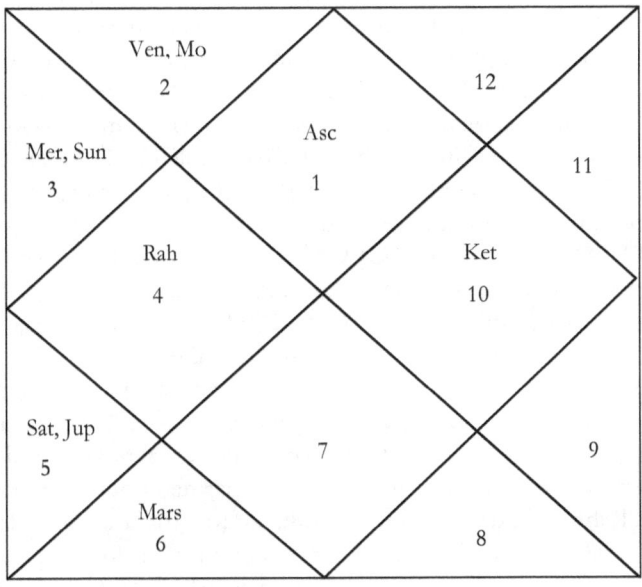

Date: July 9, 1980
Time: 1:52:00
Time Zone: 7:00:00 (West of GMT)
Place: 121 W 39' 16", 36 N 40' 40"
       Salinas, California, USA
Altitude: 53.00 meters
Ayanamsa: 23-29-18.35
Sidereal Time: 19:56:11

Jodi Arias is Aries ascendant ruled by Mars with ascendant degree at 20 degrees 20 minutes in Aries sign. In Jodi's case the ascendant lord Mars is in its worst place, in 6th house at 5 degrees 45 minutes in Virgo Sign, very close to the 6th house cusp at 5 degrees 11 minutes in Virgo Sign. In Vedic Astrology we call it a Mars affliction. Mars in 6th house is not good for conjugal happiness and this position of Mars brings violence and early death of the Love Partner. For Aries Ascendant Mars is a evil lord as it rules 1st house and 8th house at same time. Saturn is the most evil planet as it rules 11th house, the Badhaka house, and Jupiter rules the evil 12th house. Any planet connected with Mars, Saturn and Jupiter will give evil results. If we analyze Arias's astrology chart we see a connection between 5th house of love/sex lord Moon and 7th house of relationships lord Venus, as Venus and Moon are conjunct in Taurus sign in Rohini nakshatra ruled by 5th house lord Moon. This configuration is very good for love, romance and relationship. Also Rahu is very close to 5th house cusp in 5th house lord Moon's Cancer sign. This was an excellent configuration that gave her relationship with Travis Alexander during Rahu mahdasha Moon Bhukti (August 2007 to Feb 2009). But if we analyze the natal astrology chart of Jodi Arias carefully, then we see that both 5th house lord Moon and 7th house lord Venus, conjunct in Taurus sign, are aspected by Badhaka planet Saturn, by its 10th aspect from Leo sign. This configuration also indicates serious problems connected with love and with the love partner. Jodi Arias came under Rahu mahadasha, Moon Bhukti, Saturn Anthara from March 27th, 2008 to June 24th, 2008, transit Saturn at that time was transiting Leo sign and aspecting both natal Moon and natal Venus in Taurus sign, when she committed murder of her ex-boyfriend Travis Alexander on June 4th, 2008.

Jodi Arias's trial began on Jan 2nd, 2013 during Jupiter Mahadasha and Badhaka Planet Saturn's Bhukti from April 2012 to October 2014. Jodi Arias was found guilty of first degree murder on May 8th, 2013, when Bhukti lord Saturn was transiting her 7th house in Libra sign.

RELATIONSHIP COMPATIBILITY ASTROLOGY

PLANET	LONGITUDE	NAKSHATRA
ASCENDANT	20 Ar 20' 07.86"	BHARANI
SUN	23 Ge 48' 15.05"	PURNAVASU
MOON	17 Ta 09' 10.98"	ROHINI
MARS	5 Vi 45' 13.39"	U. PHALGUNI
MERCURY	27 Ge 38' 21.63"	PURNAVASU
JUPITER	13 Le 57' 04.45"	P. PHALGUNI
VENUS	22 Ta 41' 17.58"	ROHINI
SATURN(R)	28 Le 35' 09.67"	U. PHALGUNI
RAHU	28 Cn 19' 44.74"	ASLESHA
KETU	28 Cp 19' 44.74"	DHANISHTA

House	Cusp	Middle	End	Planets in it
1ST	20 Ar 20' 07.86"	4 Ta 36' 18.27"	18 Ta 52' 28.68"	ASC, MOON
2ND	18 Ta 52' 28.68"	0 Ge 07' 25.79"	11 Ge 22' 22.90"	VENUS
3RD	11 Ge 22' 22.90"	22 Ge 26' 30.25"	3 Cn 30' 37.60"	SUN, MER
4TH	3 Cn 30' 37.60"	16 Cn 36' 38.05"	29 Cn 42' 38.50"	RAHU
5TH	29 Cn 42' 38.50"	17 Le 26' 51.54"	5 Vi 11' 04.58"	JUP, SAT

6ᵀᴴ	5 Vi 11' 04.58"	27 Vi 45' 36.22"	20 Li 20' 07.86"	MARS
7ᵀᴴ	20 Li 20' 07.86"	4 Sc 36' 18.27"	18 Sc 52' 28.68"	
8ᵀᴴ	18 Sc 52' 28.68"	0 Sg 07' 25.79"	11 Sg 22' 22.90"	
9ᵀᴴ	11 Sg 22' 22.90"	22 Sg 26' 30.25"	3 Cp 30' 37.60"	
10ᵀᴴ	3 Cp 30' 37.60"	16 Cp 36' 38.05"	29 Cp 42' 38.50"	KET
11ᵀᴴ	29 Cp 42' 38.50"	17 Aq 26' 51.54"	5 Pi 11' 04.58"	
12ᵀᴴ	5 Pi 11' 04.58"	27 Pi 45' 36.22"	20 Ar 20' 07.86"	

Vimsottari Dasa:
Maha Dasas:

Moon: 1975-02-24 - 1985-02-24
Mars: 1985-02-24 - 1992-02-25
Rah: 1992-02-25 - 2010-02-24
  Antardasas in this MD:
  Rah: 1992-02-25 - 1994-11-10
  Jup: 1994-11-10 - 1997-04-01
  Sat: 1997-04-01 - 2000-02-07
  Merc: 2000-02-07 - 2002-08-29
  Ket: 2002-08-29 - 2003-09-17
  Ven: 2003-09-17 - 2006-09-17
  Sun: 2006-09-17 - 2007-08-11
  Moon: 2007-08-11 - 2009-02-06
        Pratyantardasas in this AD:
        Moon: 2007-08-11 - 2007-09-26
        Mars: 2007-09-26 - 2007-10-28
        Rah: 2007-10-28 - 2008-01-16
        Jup: 2008-01-16 - 2008-03-27
        Sat: 2008-03-27 - 2008-06-24
        Merc: 2008-06-24 - 2008-09-11

Ket: 2008-09-11 - 2008-10-14
Ven: 2008-10-14 - 2009-01-11
Sun: 2009-01-11 - 2009-02-06
Mars: 2009-02-06 - 2010-02-24
Jup: 2010-02-24 - 2026-02-24
    Antardasas in this MD:
    Jup: 2010-02-24 - 2012-04-13
    Sat: 2012-04-13 - 2014-10-29
    Merc: 2014-10-29 - 2017-01-31
    Ket: 2017-01-31 - 2018-01-08
    Ven: 2018-01-08 - 2020-09-10
    Sun: 2020-09-10 - 2021-06-27
    Moon: 2021-06-27 - 2022-10-29
    Mars: 2022-10-29 - 2023-10-05
    Rah: 2023-10-05 - 2026-02-24
Sat: 2026-02-24 - 2045-02-24
Merc: 2045-02-24 - 2062-02-25
Ket: 2062-02-25 - 2069-02-24
Ven: 2069-02-24 - 2089-02-25
Sun: 2089-02-25 - 2095-02-25

JORAN VANDER SLOOT:

Joran Andreas Petrus vander Sloot (born August 6, 1987 at 10:38 PM in Arnhem, Netherlands) is a Dutch national who lived in Aruba. He pled guilty in Peru to the murder and robbery of Stephany Tatiana Flores Ramirez, who died in the Peruviian capital on May 30, 2010. He is charged in US related to the whereabouts of Natalee Holloway, who disappeared in Aruba on May 30, 2005. On January 13, 2012, he was sentenced to 28 years imprisonment for the murder of Flores.

Date: August 6, 1987
Time: 22:38:00
Time Zone: 2:00:00 (East of GMT)
Place: 5 E 55' 00", 51 N 59' 00"
              Arnhem, Netherlands
Altitude: 0.00 meters
Ayanamsa: 23-35-14.18
Sidereal Time: 18:01:03

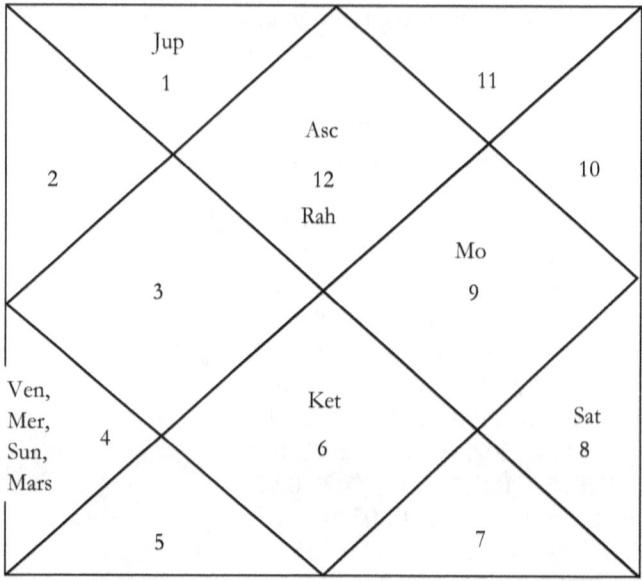

According to Vedic Astrology Joran is a Pisces ascendant ruled by Jupiter with ascendant degree at 6 degrees 54 minutes. For Pisces ascendant, the 7th house of relationships is a Badhaka house. The Ascendant lord Jupiter is in Ketu's constellation, and Ketu is placed in Badhaka house in Mercury's sign. Ketu in 7th house represents Mercury the Badhaka Planet, and Mercury is in 12th house lord Saturn's constellation. Ketu is in 5th house lord Moon's constellation, which represents sex and love affairs. As the Ascendant lord Jupiter is connected with Badhaka house, 12th house, and 5th house at same time, so the astrology chart clearly indicates involvement in sex crimes. For Pisces ascendant Mercury rules the 7th house which is the Badhaka house, a killer house. Venus rules 8th house of punishment, and Saturn rules 12th house of confinement. In Joran's astrology chart almost every planet is either in Mercury's constellation or Saturn's constellation or Venus's constellation, the three evil planets for Pisces ascendant. This indicates the person will be a killer, a very unfortunate person in life, and will spend considerable amount of time in confinement. In order for a person to spend time in prison, the significators of 3rd house (leaving one's home), 8th house

RELATIONSHIP COMPATIBILITY ASTROLOGY

(punishment by law, fine), 12th house (confinement), and of course the significators of Badhaka house must operate in their lifetime through mahadasha, Bhukti & Anthara. Joran has many planets in his astrology chart connected with these houses.

PLANET	LONGITUDE	NAKSHATRA
ASCENDANT	7 Pi 03' 28.38"	U. BHADRAPAD
SUN	20 Cn 16' 00.66"	ASLESHA
MOON	13 Sg 43' 06.40"	PURVASHADHA
MARS	26 Cn 16' 10.48"	ASLESHA
MERCURY	6 Cn 22' 18.08"	PUSHYAMI
JUPITER	5 Ar 51' 57.78"	ASWINI
VENUS	15 Cn 45' 27.69"	PUSHYAMI
SATURN(R)	21 Sc 04' 15.26"	JYESTHA
RAHU	11 Pi 22' 18.29"	U BHADRAPAD
KETU	11 Vi 22' 18.29"	HASTA

House	Cusp	Middle	End	Planets in it
1ST	7 Pi 03' 28.38"	0 Ar 55' 29.25"	24 Ar 47' 30.13"	JUP, RAHU
2ND	24 Ar 47' 30.13"	6 Ta 44' 23.84"	18 Ta 41' 17.55"	
3RD	18 Ta 41'	27 Ta 40' 16.97"	6 Ge 39' 16.38"	

		17.55"			
4TH	6 Ge 39' 16.38"	15 Ge 39' 40.55"	24 Ge 40' 04.72"	
5TH	24 Ge 40' 04.72"	6 Cn 42' 57.63"	18 Cn 45' 50.55"	MER, VENUS
6TH	18 Cn 45' 50.55"	12 Le 54' 39.46"	7 Vi 03' 28.38"	SUN, MARS
7TH	7 Vi 03' 28.38"	0 Li 55' 29.25"	24 Li 47' 30.13"	KETU
8TH	24 Li 47' 30.13"	6 Sc 44' 23.84"	18 Sc 41' 17.55"	
9TH	18 Sc 41' 17.55"	27 Sc 40' 16.97"	6 Sg 39' 16.38"	SAT
10TH	6 Sg 39' 16.38"	15 Sg 39' 40.55"	24 Sg 40' 04.72"	MOON
11TH	24 Sg 40' 04.72"	6 Cp 42' 57.63"	18 Cp 45' 50.55"	
12TH	18 Cp 45' 50.55"	12 Aq 54' 39.46"	7 Pi 03' 28.38"	

BERNIE MADDOFF:

In my case studies I also wanted to include astrology chart of a Corporate Criminal, Bernie Madoff. Bernie Madoff was born on April 29th, 1938 at 1:50 PM in New York, NY. Madoff was chairman of Bernard L Madoff Investment Securities LLC from its startup in 1960 until his arrest on Dec 11th, 2008.

Date: April 29, 1938
Time: 13:50:00
Time Zone: 4:00:00 (West of GMT)
Place: 74 W 00' 23", 40 N 42' 51"
            New York, New York, USA
Altitude: 0.00 meters
Ayanamsa: 22-53-56.72
Sidereal Time: 3:22:05

RELATIONSHIP COMPATIBILITY ASTROLOGY

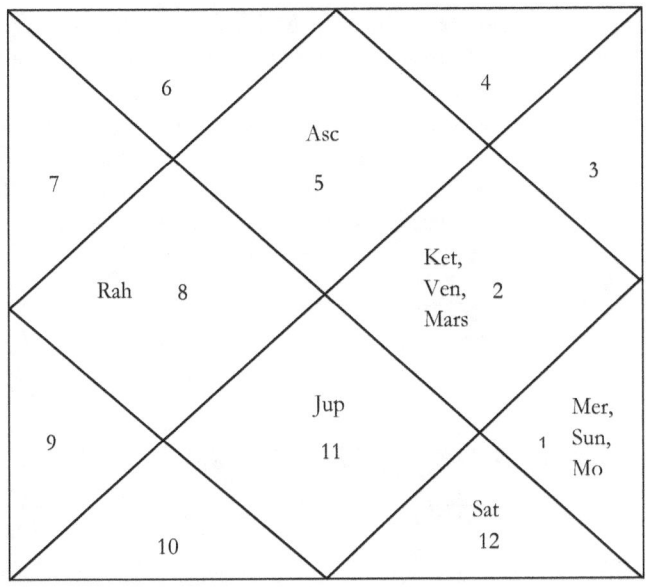

Bernie Madoff is a Leo Ascendant with Ascendant degree at 5 degrees 54 minutes in Leo sign ruled by Sun. The Ascendant Lord Sun is in 9th house, a Badhaka house for Leo Ascendant. But Sun is in excellent Nakshatra Bharani ruled by 10th house lord Venus and Venus is in 10th house. The Ascendant lord Sun's connection with 10th lord Venus gave him worldly success in a big way, but Sun's position in Badhaka house also justified that the success is based on fraud and corruption. The 7th house lord Saturn represents people who invested in Bernie's Ponzi scheme, also rules 8th house which represents his investor's money. Saturn in his chart is in 2nd and 11th house lord Mercury's nakshatra, Revathi, very good for business and money, but Mercury is again in 9th house of corruption and fraud.

Madoff entered Jupiter mahadasha in May 2001. Jupiter is a very malefic planet for Madoff, as it rules the badhaka house, the 9th house for Madoff. The 9th house cusp falls in Pisces sign at 26 degrees 54 minutes. In Jupiter mahadasha Ketu Bhukti (May 2008 to April 2009) the Ponzi scheme fell apart, as transit Jupiter was badly afflicted towards the end of 2008 and early 2009 because of its conjunction with transit Rahu in Capricorn sign. Bhukti lord Ketu was transiting Cancer Sign, in his 12th house of imprisonment.

Saturn at that time was transiting Madoff's Leo Ascendant and from there aspected both natal Jupiter in Aquarius in 7th house and natal Ketu in Taurus in his 10th house. On March 12th, 2009, Madoff pleaded guilty to 11 federal felonies and admitted to turning his wealth management business into a massive Ponzi scheme that defrauded thousands of investors of billions of dollars. On June 29th, 2009, Madoff was sentenced to 150 years in Prison.

PLANET	LONGITUDE	NAKSHATRA
ASCENDANT	5 Le 54' 60.00"	MAGHA
SUN	15 Ar 50' 55.29"	BHARANI
MOON	9 Ar 21' 37.81"	ASWINI
MARS	11 Ta 13' 15.26"	ROHINI
MERCURY	3 Ar 29' 16.48"	ASWINI
JUPITER	5 Aq 12' 06.60"	DHANISTA
VENUS	6 Ta 48' 53.57"	KRITTIKA
SATURN(R)	18 Pi 54' 35.34"	REVATI
RAHU	5 Sc 01' 22.31"	ANURADHA
KETU	5 Ta 01' 22.31"	KRITTIKA

RELATIONSHIP COMPATIBILITY ASTROLOGY

House	Cusp	Middle	End	Planets in it
1ST	5 Le 54' 60.00"	17 Le 22' 25.23"	28 Le 49' 50.46"	ASC
2ND	28 Le 49' 50.46"	12 Vi 51' 57.18"	26 Vi 54' 03.90"	
3RD	26 Vi 54' 03.90"	13 Li 27' 38.55"	0 Sc 01' 13.20"	
4TH	0 Sc 01' 13.20"	17 Sc 33' 35.23"	5 Sg 05' 57.25"	RAHU
5TH	5 Sg 05' 57.25"	21 Sg 21' 29.22"	7 Cp 37' 01.18"	
6TH	7 Cp 37' 01.18"	21 Cp 46' 00.59"	5 Aq 54' 60.00"	JUP
7TH	5 Aq 54' 60.00"	17 Aq 22' 25.23"	28 Aq 49' 50.46"	
8TH	28 Aq 49' 50.46"	12 Pi 51' 57.18"	26 Pi 54' 03.90"	SAT
9TH	26 Pi 54' 03.90"	13 Ar 27' 38.55"	0 Ta 01' 13.20"	SUN, MOON, MER
10TH	0 Ta 01' 13.20"	17 Ta 33' 35.23"	5 Ge 05' 57.25"	MARS, VEN, KETU
11TH	5 Ge 05' 57.25"	21 Ge 21' 29.22"	7 Cn 37' 01.18"	
12TH	7 Cn 37' 01.18"	21 Cn 46' 00.59"	5 Le 54' 60.00"	

Vimsottari Dasa:
Maha Dasas:
Ket: 1933-05-31 - 1940-05-31
Ven: 1940-05-31 - 1960-05-31
Sun: 1960-05-31 - 1966-05-31
Moon: 1966-05-31 - 1976-05-31
Mars: 1976-05-31 - 1983-06-01
Rah: 1983-06-01 - 2001-05-31
Jup: 2001-05-31 - 2017-05-31
    Antardasas in this MD:
    Jup: 2001-05-31 - 2003-07-21
    Sat: 2003-07-21 - 2006-01-30
    Merc: 2006-01-30 - 2008-05-06
    Ket: 2008-05-06 - 2009-04-12
    Ven: 2009-04-12 - 2011-12-14
    Sun: 2011-12-14 - 2012-10-03
    Moon: 2012-10-03 - 2014-01-30
    Mars: 2014-01-30 - 2015-01-07
    Rah: 2015-01-07 - 2017-05-31
Sat: 2017-05-31 - 2036-05-31
Merc: 2036-05-31 - 2053-06-01

BTK KILLER DENNIS LYNN RADER:

Dennis Lynn Rader (born March 9, 1945 at 2:44 PM in Wichita, Kansas) is an American serial killer and mass murderer who murdered ten people in Sedgwick County, in and around Wichita, Kansas, between 1974 and 1991. He is known as the BTK killer (or the BTK strangler). "BTK" stands for "Bind, Torture, Kill", which was his infamous signature. He is serving 10 consecutive life sentences in Kansas.

Date: March 9, 1945
Time: 14:44:00
Time Zone: 5:00:00 (West of GMT)
Place: 97 W 20' 14", 37 N 41' 32"
                Wichita, Kansas, USA
Altitude: 305.00 meters
Ayanamsa: 22-59-41.69
Sidereal Time: 0:23:10

RELATIONSHIP COMPATIBILITY ASTROLOGY

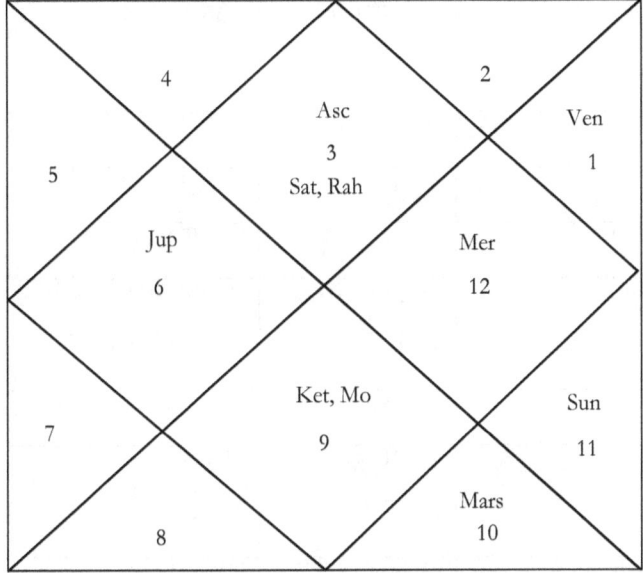

BTK Killer is a Gemini Ascendant with Ascendant degree at 28 degrees 54 minutes in Gemini sign ruled by Mercury. For Gemini Ascendant the 7th house lord Jupiter is the Badhaka Planet, Saturn rules the evil 8th house and Venus rules the 12th house of confinement. Now if we analyze the ascendant lord in BTK Killer's case, we find Mercury the ascendant ruler is in Pisces sign ruled by Badhaka Planet Jupiter and is in 8th house lord Saturn's nakshatra U Bhadrapad. Mercury in Pisces is also aspected by Badhaka Planet Jupiter in Virgo sign, and the 8th house ruler Saturn from Gemini also aspects natal Mercury in Pisces, by its 10th aspect. The ascendant lord Mercury has a strong connection with Badhaka Planet Jupiter and 8th house lord Saturn. Hence the person is a BTK killer.

GURMEET SINGH

PLANET	LONGITUDE	NAKSHATRA
ASCENDANT	28 Ge 54' 28.63"	PURNAVASU
SUN	25 Aq 53' 41.74"	P BHADRAPAD
MOON	27 Sg 21' 32.02"	UTTARASHADHA
MARS	25 Cp 06' 10.31"	DHANISTHA
MERCURY	4 Pi 11' 25.16"	U BHADRAPAD
JUPITER	0 Vi 03' 38.07"	U PHALGUNI
VENUS	6 Ar 11' 16.11"	ASWINI
SATURN(R)	10 Ge 51' 20.15"	ARDRA
RAHU	22 Ge 13' 13.94"	PURNAVASU
KETU	22 Sg 13' 13.94"	PURVASHADHA

House	Cusp	Middle	End	Planets in it
1ST	28 Ge 54' 28.63"	9 Cn 11' 35.70"	19 Cn 28' 42.76"	ASC
2ND	19 Cn 28' 42.76"	1 Le 27' 05.48"	13 Le 25' 28.21"	
3RD	13 Le 25' 28.21"	28 Le 22' 08.10"	13 Vi 18' 47.98"	JUP
4TH	13 Vi 18' 47.98"	1 Li 20' 51.85"	19 Li 22' 55.71"	
5TH	19 Li 22'	7 Sc 56' 29.90"	26 Sc 30' 04.08"	

RELATIONSHIP COMPATIBILITY ASTROLOGY

			55.71"		
6ᵀᴴ	26 Sc 30' 04.08"		12 Sg 42' 16.36"	28 Sg 54' 28.63"	MOON, KETU
7ᵀᴴ	28 Sg 54' 28.63"		9 Cp 11' 35.70"	19 Cp 28' 42.76"	
8ᵀᴴ	19 Cp 28' 42.76"		1 Aq 27' 05.48"	13 Aq 25' 28.21"	MARS
9ᵀᴴ	13 Aq 25' 28.21"		28 Aq 22' 08.10"	13 Pi 18' 47.98"	SUN, MER
10ᵀᴴ	13 Pi 18' 47.98"		1 Ar 20' 51.85"	19 Ar 22' 55.71"	VENUS
11ᵀᴴ	19 Ar 22' 55.71"		7 Ta 56' 29.90"	26 Ta 30' 04.08"	
12ᵀᴴ	26 Ta 30' 04.08"		12 Ge 42' 16.36"	28 Ge 54' 28.63"	SAT, RAHU

Vimsottari Dasa:
Maha Dasas:
Sun: 1944-11-18 - 1950-11-19
Moon: 1950-11-19 - 1960-11-19
Mars: 1960-11-19 - 1967-11-19
Rah: 1967-11-19 - 1985-11-19
Jup: 1985-11-19 - 2001-11-19
Sat: 2001-11-19 - 2020-11-19
Merc: 2020-11-19 - 2037-11-19
Ket: 2037-11-19 - 2044-11-19
Ven: 2044-11-19 - 2064-11-19

PHIL SPECTOR:

Phil Spector (born December 26, 1939 at 2:55 PM in Bronx, New York) is an American record producer, song writer, and the originator of the "Wall of Sound" production method. Spector was a pioneer of the 1960s girl-group sound, and produced more than twenty-five Top 40 hits from 1960 to 1965 at the height of his career. In 2009, Spector was convicted of second-degree murder in the 2003 shooting death of actress Lana Clarkson in his Alhambra California home. He is serving a prison sentence of 19 years to life.

Date: December 26, 1939
Time: 14:55:00
Time Zone: 5:00:00 (West of GMT)
Place: 73 W 52' 00", 40 N 51' 00"
            Bronx, New York, USA
Altitude: 120.00 meters
Ayanamsa: 22-55-20.15
Sidereal Time: 21:17:11

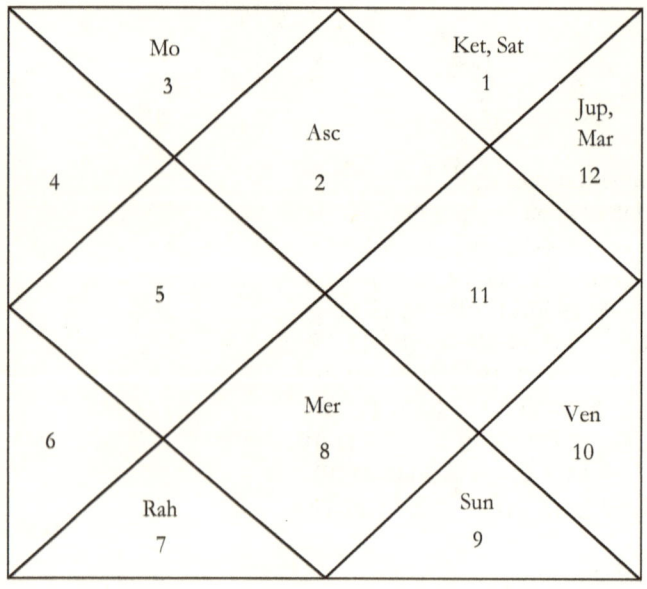

Phil Spector is a Taurus ascendant ruled by Venus, with ascendant degree at 18 degrees 32 minutes in Taurus sign. For Taurus ascendant the evil lord are Mars, Jupiter and Saturn, as Mars rules the 12th house of confinement, Jupiter rules the 8th house of punishment, and Saturn being the 9th house lord is the Badhaka planet. If we analyze the ascendant lord Venus we can easily see criminal and violent tendencies in the astrology chart. Venus, the ascendant lord is positioned in the Badhaka (9th) house in Capricorn sign in Spector's natal astrology chart, and is aspected by the Badhaka Planet Saturn by its 10th aspect from Aries sign. The ascendant lord Venus also has a connection with the 5th house lord Sun (the 5th house cusp is in Leo sign), by being in Uttarashada nakshatra ruled by Sun in Capricorn sign. The connection with Sun gave him celebrity status.

On February 3, 2003, actress Lana Clarkson was found dead in Spector's mansion in Alhambra, California, while Spector was in Ketu mahadasha, Saturn Bhukti, and Moon Anthara. In the natal chart Ketu is in 12th house, in its own nakshatra Aswini, and is very closely conjunct Badhaka Planet Saturn. Natal moon is in Rahu's nakshatra, Ardra in Gemini sign in second house. Natal Rahu is again aspected by Badhaka Planet Saturn and Rahu is in 12th house lord Mars nakshatra Chitra. At the time of murder mahadasha lord Ketu was transiting Scorpio sign in Spector's 7th house in Badhaka Planet Saturn's anuradha nakshatra. Bhukti lord Saturn was with Rahu in the ascendant sign Taurus by transit, and the 7th house lord Mars was in Scorpio sign with mahadasha lord Ketu.

Spector was found guilty of the second degree murder, and Jury returned a guilty verdict on April 13, 2009 when Spector was in Venus mahdasha, Moon Bhukti and Rahu Anthara. According to documents filed by the prosecution, Spector had previously pulled a gun on four women he dated. In each case, he had been drinking and "was romantically interested in the woman, but grew angry after the woman spurned him". This behavior is clearly indicated in Spector's astrology chart.

GURMEET SINGH

PLANET	LONGITUDE	NAKSHATRA
ASCENDANT	18 Ta 32' 03.41"	ROHINI
SUN	11 Sg 13' 56.51"	MOOLA
MOON	15 Ge 53' 10.96"	ARDRA
MARS	1 Pi 32' 51.61"	P BHADRAPAD
MERCURY	21 Sc 58' 18.03"	JYESTHA
JUPITER	7 Pi 39' 30.53"	U BHADRAPAD
VENUS	8 Cp 58' 22.78"	UTTARASHADHA
SATURN(R)	1 Ar 29' 32.92"	ASWINI
RAHU	2 Li 54' 18.24"	CHITRA
KETU	2 Ar 54' 18.24"	ASWINI

House	Cusp	Middle	End	Planets in it
1ST	18 Ta 32' 03.41"	29 Ta 36' 51.75"	10 Ge 41' 40.08"	ASC
2ND	10 Ge 41' 40.08"	20 Ge 52' 38.51"	1 Cn 03' 36.94"	MOON
3RD	1 Cn 03' 36.94"	12 Cn 29' 23.73"	23 Cn 55' 10.52"	
4TH	23 Cn 55' 10.52"	8 Le 51' 22.46"	23 Le 47' 34.41"	
5TH	23 Le 47' 34.41"	14 Vi 09' 45.20"	4 Li 31' 55.99"	RAHU

6TH	4 Li 31' 55.99"	26 Li 31' 59.70"	18 Sc 32' 03.41"	
7TH	18 Sc 32' 03.41"	29 Sc 36' 51.75"	10 Sg 41' 40.08"	MER
8TH	10 Sg 41' 40.08"	20 Sg 52' 38.51"	1 Cp 03' 36.94"	SUN
9TH	1 Cp 03' 36.94"	12 Cp 29' 23.73"	23 Cp 55' 10.52"	VEN
10TH	23 Cp 55' 10.52"	8 Aq 51' 22.46"	23 Aq 47' 34.41"	
11TH	23 Aq 47' 34.41"	14 Pi 09' 45.20"	4 Ar 31' 55.99"	MARS, JUP, SAT, KETU
12TH	4 Ar 31' 55.99"	26 Ar 31' 59.70"	18 Ta 32' 03.41"	

Vimsottari Dasa:
Maha Dasas:
    Rah: 1927-07-16 - 1945-07-16
    Jup: 1945-07-16 - 1961-07-16
    Sat: 1961-07-16 - 1980-07-16
    Merc: 1980-07-16 - 1997-07-16
    Ket: 1997-07-16 - 2004-07-16
        Antardasas in this MD:
        Ket: 1997-07-16 - 1997-12-12
        Ven: 1997-12-12 - 1999-02-10
        Sun: 1999-02-10 - 1999-06-18
        Moon: 1999-06-18 - 2000-01-17
        Mars: 2000-01-17 - 2000-06-14
        Rah: 2000-06-14 - 2001-07-03
        Jup: 2001-07-03 - 2002-06-09
        Sat: 2002-06-09 - 2003-07-20
        Merc: 2003-07-20 - 2004-07-16
    Ven: 2004-07-16 - 2024-07-16
        Antardasas in this MD:
        Ven: 2004-07-16 - 2007-11-16

　　　　Sun: 2007-11-16 - 2008-11-16
　　　　Moon: 2008-11-16 - 2010-07-16
　　　　Mars: 2010-07-16 - 2011-09-17
　　　　Rah: 2011-09-17 - 2014-09-17
　　　　Jup: 2014-09-17 - 2017-05-14
　　　　Sat: 2017-05-14 - 2020-07-16
　　　　Merc: 2020-07-16 - 2023-05-15
　　　　Ket: 2023-05-15 - 2024-07-16
　Sun: 2024-07-16 - 2030-07-16
　Moon: 2030-07-16 - 2040-07-16
　Mars: 2040-07-16 - 2047-07-17

In this chapter you have learnt how by analyzing a Potential Partner's astrology chart you can understand their personality, character, criminal and violent tendencies before you enter into a Love or Business Relationship with them. For Chara (Movable) ascendants, the ascendant lord is strong if it is connected to houses 1-2-3-5-10-9-6, their prosperity in life will be of high level. For Sthira (Fixed) ascendants, the ascendant lord is strong if it is connected to houses 1-2-3-5-10-11-6, their prosperity in life will be of high level. For Ubhaya (Common) ascendants, the ascendant lord is strong if it is connected to houses 2-3-6-11-5-9 their prosperity in life will be of high level.

8 BUSINESS COMPATIBILITY

Astrological Compatibility is a way to get the knowledge regarding the nature, character, and the social communication features of the people, you want to enter into a business partnership. Unless and until compatibility is found between the two persons, they can't hold healthy relationship. Since it is very difficult to get knowledge on the potential partner's nature, potential to generate financial wealth etc. before entering into the business partnership, astrology can definitely help you in knowing the astrological probability of growing your business together with your business partner. Astrology helps you to find out whether you should start or continue the partnership with your partner or not as it helps you to figure out your levels of astrological compatibility with your partner. Business Compatibility Astrology will help you understand the overall compatibility between business partners. Whether similar luck pattern would operate in the future to ensure that you would be working together on a long term basis. Whether partnership business suits both or all partners at the same time? It is important to know if your business is compatible with you. In a recent research conducted into the lives of over 500 millionaires in the world, it was found that most of these millionaires were people who were either working or running their businesses in areas that they found interesting and compatible with their natural gifts and talents. These people had found their "niche" in life and focused their efforts on succeeding within those niches or positions. However, poor or average people do just the opposite. They spend most of their time doing jobs that they hate or running businesses in areas for which they have no talent. And they experience defeat and failure. It is just as important to understand if your business partner is truly a compatible match or not. This is especially important if you are working as partners in the business.

Partnerships play a pivotal role in any commercial enterprise. The type and quality of a partnership can make or break a business. The stars of your partners affect your future and vice versa. Therefore, it is of crucial importance for the success of your business to determine whether the stars of partners are compatible or not, whether the person you want to start your business with is right one? Many times an enterprise hit the rocks due to just one business partner. And the cause might be lack of compatibility or difference in thinking patterns or incoherent temperaments of the partners etc. A good partnership brings great success and earns reward from the field of business. On the other hand due to the bad partnership, one may face failure and loss in business. You can avoid it all by getting a Business Compatibility Profile based on the Natal Chart of the partners involved in the Business. Whether you're starting up, starting over, or trying to take your business to the next level, there isn't any aspect of business that doesn't involve human relationships. From choosing business partners to hiring employees to evaluating potential clients, compatible business relationships are crucial. But too many of us choose the wrong people for the wrong reasons—often emotional ones—and by doing so undermine a key building block of business success. Relationship Compatibility Astrology can help you find the right Business Partner. My clients ask questions in Business Compatibility readings, 'Are we good business partners'? 'Will our working relationship be successful'? 'Should we start business together'? Can astrology answer these questions? The answer is, yes astrology can definitely help to answer all such questions about your business partnership. In your business partnerships compatibility readings, I will figure out your levels of astrological compatibility with your partner, whether you should start or continue the partnership with that person. You are about to start a business and want to know if your partner is trustworthy? Is the partnership going to be fruitful or disastrous? If you are single and are thinking about getting involved with someone, it is very worthwhile to get the birth data of a prospective partner. Astrology can also provide insights into ongoing relationships such as pointing out periods of particular tension or harmony, general luck of each partner, temperament compatibility to each other, chances of success, when and to what level, any chances of cheating and fraud in the business partnership, any chances of working together on a long term basis etc. Any business under partnership succeeds when partners are compatible with each other.

We already had detailed discussions on the 'Violent and Criminal tendencies in the astrology chart' in chapter 7, that will help the readers to find out temperament compatibility of business partners to each other, any chances of cheating and fraud in the business partnership. In this chapter we will have detailed discussions on three important questions in Relationship Compatibility Astrology for Business. Is the astrology chart good for business? Is the astrology chart good for generating Financial Wealth? Is the astrology chart of each business partner compatible for Business with the other Business Partners?

Is the astrology chart good for business?

The 7th house in the astrology chart represents business, business partners, clients and customers who will buy your product. 7th house represents your competitors and enemies as well. In my opinion people are inclined to start business when they are going through the mahadasha or bhukti of planets connected with the 7th house. In the astrology chart if the cuspal sub lord of the 10th house is the significator of the 2nd, 7th, or 10th, an independent business or profession is promised during the joint period of the significators of the 2nd, 7th, and 10th. If the cuspal sub lord of the 7th is the significator of the 2nd, 10th or 11th, gain in business is promised during the joint period of the significators of the 2nd, 10th, and 11th. The 7th house is dealings with others, purchase and sale of production; it is the main house for business. If the sub lord of the 7th cusp is connected with the 8th or 12th or Badhaka house, one loses. The business winds up due to loss, if the lord of 7th house is in the sub of a planet who is occupying the 8th or 12th or Badhaka house or the lord of 7th house is deposited in the constellation of a planet connected with the 8th or 12th or Badhaka house. If the star lord of the 10 cusp lord is connected to 6-8-12 then paid job is suitable. But if the star lord of the 10th cusp lord is connected with the 1-7-10-11 then independent business is suitable. If the Cuspal sub lord of the 7th be the significator of 8 or 12, the native will suffer loss in business during the joint period of the significators of 8 and 12.

Is the astrology chart good for generating Financial Wealth?

The second house cuspal position determines whether one will earn enormous wealth, or earn to a middle level, or earn a low level income.

If the 2nd house cuspal position is connected to 5-8-12 house, the native is poor.

If the 2nd house cuspal position is connected to 5-8-12 houses along with 2-11 the native is middle class.

If the 2nd house cuspal position is connected to 2-10-11, without any connections to 5-8-12 the native is above middle class.

If the 2nd house cuspal position is connected to 2-6-10-11, with no connections at all to 5-8-12, the native makes enormous wealth.

Consider houses 2, 6, 10 and 11 for gain of money in any manner. Houses 8, 12, and Badhaka indicates loss of money, obstacles, and poverty. When any planet is the significator of 8, 12, or Badhaka that planet can causes loss of money and poverty.. Planets posted in the constellations of the occupants in the houses 2, 6, 10, 11 are the strongest to give wealth to a person. These planets may be debilitated or in enemy's house. Still one's status will improve in their periods and sub periods. Planets posted in the constellations of the lords of the houses 2, 6, 10, 11 are also stronger to give wealth to a person. If most of the planets in an astrology chart are connected with the 2nd, 6th, 10th, 11th house, the astrology chart is good for generating financial wealth. But if most of the planets in an astrology chart are connected with the 8th, 12th, and Badhaka house then it indicates loss of money, and poverty.

Is the astrology chart for each business partner compatible for Business with the other Business Partners?

After ensuring that each business partner's astrology chart is good for business, and promises good financial wealth in the coming years after they incorporate their business relationship, the next thing we want analyze is the business compatibility between different business partners. If you remember our discussions on 'Sexual Compatibility' in chapter 3, the focus was more on the 5th house and 7th house, because 5th house represents bed pleasures, intimacy and sex, the 7th house represents relationships and marriage. Over there you were looking for a love partner, who is good for intimacy and bed pleasures. In Business Compatibility the focus is more on the generation of financial wealth for yourself and your business partners by working together as business partners in a Business Enterprise. The 2nd house in the astrology chart represents your bank balance and your ability to generate financial wealth. The 11th house is the house of gains, 10th house is your position, status, career in life, and 6th house is the house of competition, gains to you and loss to your competitors. So the 2nd, 6th, 10th and 11th houses are the houses of financial prosperity. The 8th house, 12th house and the Badhaka houses represent loss, grief, deception, punishment by law, and violence. As I mentioned before the people you meet in your daily life, including your business partners, are all represented by planets in your astrology chart. If a planet is evil in your astrology chart because of its connection with the 8th house, 12th house or Badhaka house, the planet is not going to come down from sky to harm you, the evil planet will send someone in your life, may be a business partner, who is represented by that evil planet, and you suffer loss, deception, and grief through that business partner. You should never have a business partner who is represented by the Badhaka house in your astrology chart or vice versa as it can bring violence in the business relationship. On the flip side if your business partner is represented by a planet connected with a financial wealth generating house, such as the 2nd house or 11th house in your astrology chart, then the business partner is represented by a very auspicious wealth generating planet in your astrology chart, this business partner can bring good luck and financial prosperity for you. If you can find such compatibility in the astrology charts of both or all business partners, then the business compatibility exists both ways, it is a win, win situation for both or all business partners. But most of the time the Business Compatibility exists one way, business partner B is very lucky for business partner A but not vice versa.

Next we will do couple of case studies. I have taken two astrology charts - one represents a person who lost everything in business and the other a Billionaire. We will analyze why one is poor and lost everything in business and the other a Billionaire. We will also see how Saturn completely destroyed the career / business of one person because it ruled the Badhaka house, and many natal planets, were connected with the Badhaka planet Saturn. On the flip side the same Saturn made the other person a Billionaire because Saturn ruled the 2nd house of money in the astrology chart, and many planets were connected with the 2nd lord Saturn in the astrology chart. We will also analyze what kind of business partners are compatible with both for business, and what kind of business partners will bring loss, deception and fraud in the business partnership for these astrology charts.

CASE STUDY 1

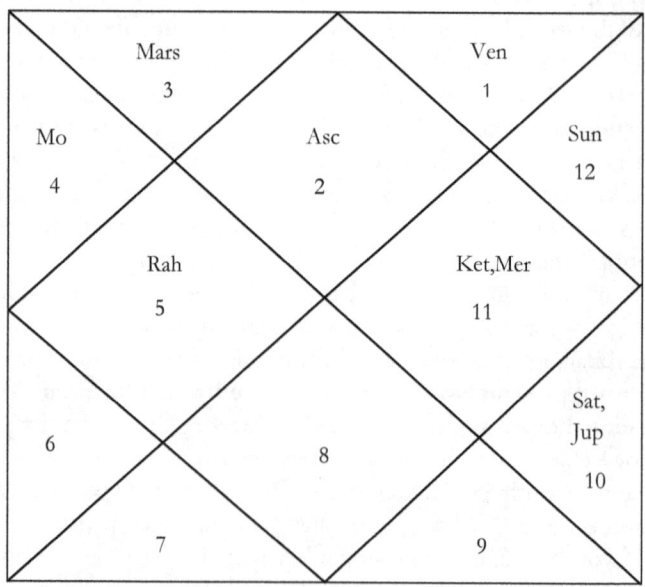

This person is a Taurus ascendant with ascendant at 15 degrees in Taurus sign ruled by Venus. For Taurus ascendant the three evil lords are – Jupiter rules the 8th house, Mars rules the 12th house and the 9th house lord Saturn is the Badhaka planet. If we analyze the natal planets in this astrology chart we will find that many planets are connected with the Badhaka house lord Saturn. 3rd and 4th house lord Moon is stationed in Cancer sign, in Pushyami nakshatra ruled Badhaka planet Saturn, and Moon is badly aspected by the Badhaka planet Saturn and the 8th house lord Jupiter. 5th house lord Sun is in Pisces sign in 11th house in the U. Bhadrapad nakshatra ruled by Badhaka planet Saturn, and Sun is badly aspected by the Badhaka planet Saturn. Badhaka planet Saturn rules 9th, 10th, and 11th house and is stationed in the 9th house in Capricorn sign in the Uttarashadha nakshatra ruled by 5th house lord Sun and Sun is again aspected by the badhaka planet Saturn. 8th house lord Jupiter is in Conjunction with the Badhaka planet Saturn, and Jupiter is also stationed in the 9th house in Capricorn sign in the Uttarashadha nakshatra ruled by 5th house lord Sun, and Sun is again aspected by the Badhaka planet Saturn. Mars rules the 12th house of loss, and aspects both Jupiter and Saturn by its 8th aspect. The ascendant lord Venus is very close to the 12th house cusp in Aswini nakshatra ruled by Ketu. Ketu in 10th represents Badhaka planet Saturn, by being in Saturn's sign Aquarius. Venus the ascendant lord is also evil, connected with the 12th house and the Badhaka house. The only good planets I see are Mercury, and Rahu, as 2nd house lord Mercury aspects Rahu, and Ketu to some extent is also good, by being in conjunction with the 2nd house lord Mercury. This person was born in a decent, well to do family, and things were going well in his life when he was in Mercury mahadasha and Ketu mahadasha. He became business partner in his father's business in Venus mahadasha. As we know father is represented by 9th house in the astrology chart. In this chart the 9th house lord Saturn is a Badhaka planet, and it represents father. He consulted many traditional vedic astrologers at that time, they all predicted great things for him in business, because according to them the 9th house is the house of luck and fortune. Some vedic astrologers even asked him to try the Saturn stone, blue sapphire. He followed their advice and was wearing a big blue sapphire. In my opinion this blue sapphire gave more power to evil Saturn, the ruler of Badhaka house, and caused more harm to him. These traditional vedic astrologers did not know that for Taurus ascendant, Saturn is the worst planet, if the 9th house cusp falls in Saturn Sign, because 9th house is the Badhaka house for Taurus ascendant. In Venus mahdasha Saturn Bhukti from July 1998 to September 2001, the business failed miserably, and both son and the father were in deep debt, and they lost all their money and assets. Transit Saturn at that time was transiting in his 12th house in Aries sign, directly over the natal Venus. Saturn from Aries sign also aspected the natal position of the 7th house lord Mars in Gemini sign by its 3rd aspect, and natal Saturn & Jupiter by its 10th aspect. This astrology chart has many planets connected with the Badhaka house, 12th house, and 8th house. I would have never recommended business for this person. The only good planets I see are the 2nd house lord Mercury, and Rahu. I would have recommended 'Green Emerald' stone that represents 2nd lord Mercury for this person for good luck. In my opinion a Gemini ascendant and Ardra nakshatra ruled by Rahu would have been compatible for any kind of partnership with this person. But this astrology chart has many weak planets, and business is not recommended for this person.

PLANET	LONGITUDE	NAKSHATRA
ASCENDANT	14 Ta 58' 20.49"	ROHINI
SUN	13 Pi 03' 18.34"	U BHADRAPAD
MOON	16 Cn 20' 54.91"	PUSHYAMI
MARS	18 Ge 14' 52.26"	ARDRA
MERCURY	16 Aq 12' 11.53"	SATABHISHA
JUPITER	8 Cp 48' 05.46"	UTTARASHADHA
VENUS	5 Ar 02' 55.28"	ASWINI
SATURN(R)	5 Cp 08' 33.49"	UTTARASHADHA
RAHU	11 Le 36' 54.99"	MAGHA
KETU	11 Aq 36' 54.99"	SATABHISHA

RELATIONSHIP COMPATIBILITY ASTROLOGY

House	Cusp	Middle	End	Planets in it
1ST	14 Ta 58' 20.49"	27 Ta 17' 59.08"	9 Ge 37' 37.68"	ASC
2ND	9 Ge 37' 37.68"	21 Ge 16' 01.68"	2 Cn 54' 25.69"	MARS
3RD	2 Cn 54' 25.69"	15 Cn 45' 47.97"	28 Cn 37' 10.25"	MOON
4TH	28 Cn 37' 10.25"	14 Le 17' 03.37"	29 Le 56' 56.49"	RAHU
5TH	29 Le 56' 56.49"	18 Vi 37' 50.13"	7 Li 18' 43.77"	
6TH	7 Li 18' 43.77"	26 Li 08' 32.13"	14 Sc 58' 20.49"	
7TH	14 Sc 58' 20.49"	27 Sc 17' 59.08"	9 Sg 37' 37.68"	
8TH	9 Sg 37' 37.68"	21 Sg 16' 01.68"	2 Cp 54' 25.69"	
9TH	2 Cp 54' 25.69"	15 Cp 45' 47.97"	28 Cp 37' 10.25"	JUP, SAT
10TH	28 Cp 37' 10.25"	14 Aq 17' 03.37"	29 Aq 56' 56.49"	MER, KETU
11TH	29 Aq 56' 56.49"	18 Pi 37' 50.13"	7 Ar 18' 43.77"	SUN, VENUS
12TH	7 Ar 18' 43.77"	26 Ar 08' 32.13"	14 Ta 58' 20.49"	

Vimsottari Dasa:
Maha Dasas:
Sat: 1942-09-12 - 1961-09-12
Merc: 1961-09-12 - 1978-09-13
Ket: 1978-09-13 - 1985-09-12
Ven: 1985-09-12 - 2005-09-12
    Antar Dasa:
    Ven: 1985-09-12 - 1989-01-10
    Sun: 1989-01-10 - 1990-01-10
    Moon: 1990-01-10 - 1991-09-13
    Mars: 1991-09-13 - 1992-11-12
    Rah: 1992-11-12 - 1995-11-13
    Jup: 1995-11-13 - 1998-07-12
    Sat: 1998-07-12 - 2001-09-12 (BUSINESS FAILED, LOST EVERYTHING)
    Merc: 2001-09-12 - 2004-07-12
    Ket: 2004-07-12 - 2005-09-12
Sun: 2005-09-12 - 2011-09-13
Moon: 2011-09-13 - 2021-09-13
Mars: 2021-09-13 - 2028-09-12
Rah: 2028-09-12 - 2046-09-13
Jup: 2046-09-13 - 2062-09-13

CASE STUDY 2

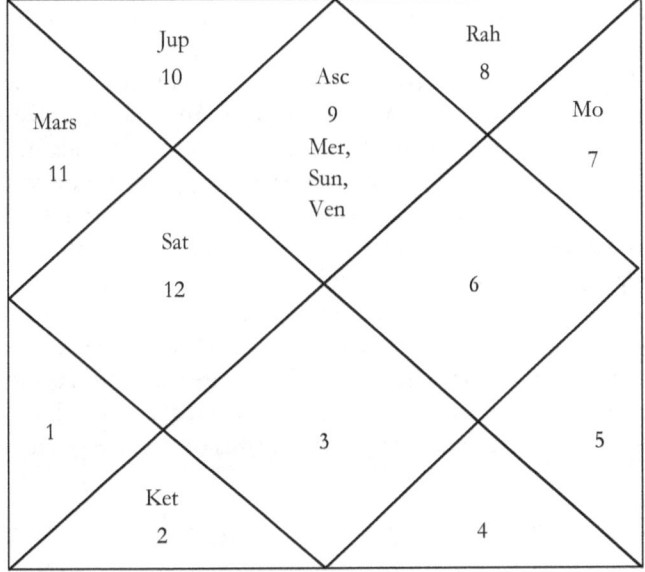

This is the astrology chart of a Billionaire. He is Sagittarius ascendant with ascendant degree at 3 degrees 05 minutes in moola nakshatra ruled by Ketu in Sagittarius sign ruled by Jupiter. The lord of financial wealth, that is 2nd house lord is Saturn. We will see that there is a strong 2nd house lord Saturn influence in this astrology chart. The second house cusp lord is Saturn in this case as the second house cusp fall in Capricorn sign at 4 degrees, 14 minutes in Uttarashadha nakshatra ruled by Sun and is in the sub of Saturn, clearly indicates enormous financial wealth. Saturn, the most auspicious planet in this astrology chart rules 2nd and 3rd house and is in its own nakshatra U. Bhadrapad in Pisces sign. We see the 2nd house lord Saturn is aspecting natal Ketu in Taurus sign by its 3rd aspect, and Sun, Mercury, Venus in Sagittarius by its 10th aspect. The ascendant lord Jupiter is in 2nd house of money, in Capricorn sign ruled by Saturn, in the nakshatra of Uttarashadha ruled by 9th house lord Sun, and Sun is aspected by 2nd lord Saturn by its 10th aspect. Rahu is in 12th house in Scorpio sign ruled by 12th house lord Mars, but in the Anuradha nakshatra ruled by 2nd lord

Saturn. Moon the ruler of 8th house is in the 11th house, in the vishaka nakshatra ruled by ascendant and 4th house lord Jupiter and Jupiter is stationed in the 2nd house of money. So many planets connected with the house of money that is 2nd house lord Saturn, and the person is a billionaire. This person can experience financial gains by having business partnership with someone ruled by Saturn or Jupiter, or Venus, such as Capricorn or Aquarius ascendant or Sagittarius or Pisces ascendant or Libra or Taurus ascendant. This person should avoid business partnership with someone who is ruled by 12th house lord Mars, such as Scorpio or Aries ascendant, 8th house lord Moon ascendant or badhaka planet Mercury as ascendant lord, such as Gemini or Virgo ascendant as these ascendants will not be compatible for business because of their connection with the evil houses in the astrology chart. I will recommend 'Blue Sapphire' stone that represents the auspicious planet Saturn the ruler of second house and 'Yellow Sapphire' that represents the ascendant lord Jupiter for this person for good luck.

PLANET	LONGITUDE	NAKSHATRA
ASCENDANT	3 Sg 05' 19.90"	MOOLA
SUN	12 Sg 59' 37.43"	MOOLA
MOON	21 Li 43' 46.33"	VISHAKA
MARS	11 Aq 52' 43.45"	SATABHISHA
MERCURY	17 Sg 51' 12.13"	PURVASHADHA
JUPITER	8 Cp 51' 04.27"	UTTARASHADHA
VENUS	3 Sg 52' 45.89"	MOOLA
SATURN(R)	6 Pi 03' 46.50"	U BHADRAPAD
RAHU	11 Sc 31' 30.10"	ANURADHA
KETU	11 Ta 31' 30.10"	ROHINI

RELATIONSHIP COMPATIBILITY ASTROLOGY

House	Cusp	Middle	End	Planets in it
1ST	3 Sg 05' 19.90"	18 Sg 39' 47.19"	4 Cp 14' 14.48"	ASC, SUN, MER, VENUS
2ND	4 Cp 14' 14.48"	21 Cp 04' 48.79"	7 Aq 55' 23.10"	JUP
3RD	7 Aq 55' 23.10"	24 Aq 47' 10.13"	11 Pi 38' 57.17"	MARS, SAT
4TH	11 Pi 38' 57.17"	26 Pi 50' 03.60"	12 Ar 01' 10.04"	
5TH	12 Ar 01' 10.04"	25 Ar 15' 19.64"	8 Ta 29' 29.23"	
6TH	8 Ta 29' 29.23"	20 Ta 47' 24.57"	3 Ge 05' 19.90"	KETU
7TH	3 Ge 05' 19.90"	18 Ge 39' 47.19"	4 Cn 14' 14.48"	
8TH	4 Cn 14' 14.48"	21 Cn 04' 48.79"	7 Le 55' 23.10"	
9TH	7 Le 55' 23.10"	24 Le 47' 10.13"	11 Vi 38' 57.17"	
10TH	11 Vi 38' 57.17"	26 Vi 50' 03.60"	12 Li 01' 10.04"	
11TH	12 Li 01' 10.04"	25 Li 15' 19.64"	8 Sc 29' 29.23"	MOON
12TH	8 Sc 29' 29.23"	20 Sc 47' 24.57"	3 Sg 05' 19.90"	RAHU

ABOUT THE AUTHOR

Gurmeet Singh is an internationally acclaimed Vedic Astrologer with over 25 years of experience as a full time consulting astrologer in Advanced Vedic Astrology (KP System). Mr. Singh is one of the most respected astrologers in America who is experienced and practiced in Vedic Astrology and Stellar Astrology. He is a long standing member of the astrological community in the Beverly Hills / Los Angeles California metropolitan areas. Mr. Singh is an expert on the usage of Nakshatras, which gives much more accurate predictions than the usage of house ruler ship, as there are 27 Nakshatras (Constellations) and 249 subs, but only 12 houses in the Zodiac. Mr. Singh is expert on Relationship Compatibility issues, and can tell which ascendant signs are compatible with you for a romantic or business relationship, and which ascendant signs will bring loss, sorrow, grief and deception to you. Singh was born in India, and raised in US. He became interested in Vedic Astrology at the age of twelve. Singh had deep interest in complex subjects such as Science, Math, and Astrology. Singh holds a masters degree in Computer Science from Wayne State University, Detroit, Michigan.

Mr. Singh consults on Vedic Astrology throughout the world. In over two decades Mr. Singh has read tens of thousands of astrological charts. His clients include celebrities, professional astrologers, business professionals, and politicians. Mr. Singh maintains a busy Vedic Astrology practice in Los Angeles California, where he is consulted by people for Vedic Astrology Readings from all over the world, and from all walks of life. Don't be shy; feel free to contact Mr. Singh at gsingh9186@aol.com or via his website www.vedicnakshatras.com. Mr. Singh would love to hear from you.

www.ingramcontent.com/pod-product-compliance
Lightning Source LLC
Chambersburg PA
CBHW021846220426
43663CB00005B/429